Praise fo

"This is a fun chick lit i. sleuth supported by an eccentric bunch of BBs (baby boomers), the cop and the daughter. Carol tells the tale in an amusing frantic way that adds to the enjoyment of a fine lighthearted whodunit that affirms that "every wife has a story."

–Harriet Klausner, national book critic

"The over-50 crowd will love this....I love this lighthearted mystery. Susan Santangelo combines humor and mystery to create a great read. I am so glad to see a female lead character over 50....This is a must read!"

–Readers' Favorite

"Not since picking up one of Janet Evanovich's Stephanie Plum books have I ever laughed or enjoyed a book so much as Susan Santangelo's ***Retirement Can Be Murder***."

–Suspense Magazine

"Santangelo ... captures well the anxiety of a wife who must face the reality of her life turning upside down. Good thing she has her friends to help."

–Blog Critics

"Finally a cozy mystery with a heroine who's middle-aged, married, and a mother....What really makes ***Retirement Can Be Murder*** special is the author's uncanny knack for finding humor in everyday situations.... One of the funniest cozies I've ever read, and yet all of the humor flows naturally from the characters, the plot, and the dialogue."

–Patricia Rockwell, Author of *Sounds of Murder*

"Susan Santangelo may be the next Jessica Fletcher, the mystery writer and amateur detective portrayed by Angela Lansbury in the award-winning television series *Murder She Wrote*.... Susan's found a niche in the mystery-writing genre that just might find its way to the television screen, judging by the popularity of her first book, ***Retirement Can Be Murder***."

–Shoreline Times

"***Moving Can Be Murder*** is jam-packed with Carol's cast of best buds and signature Santangelo fun! The author has penned a magnificent cozy that will leave you panting from the excitement, laughing at the characters, and – no surprise here – begging for more."

–*Terri Ann Armstrong,* Author of *How To Plant A Body*

"Not only is ***Moving Can Be Murder*** fun to read, it also includes valuable hints at the end if you're thinking of moving. Thanks, Susan, for another excellent mystery!"

–*Marie Sherman,* Author of *Say I Do! Tales of a Cape Cod Justice of the Peace*

"***Marriage Can Be Murder*** is filled with humor, interesting characters, and life's complexities....It's a winning selection to beat the blues or the blahs."

–*Technorati.com*

"***Marriage Can Be Murder***, the third in a series by Susan Santangelo, is a clever and amusing story involving a couple who get tangled up in solving mysteries when they aren't busy driving each other crazy as they get used to retirement. Pure enjoyment."

–*Carole Goldberg,* former Books Editor, *Hartford Courant*

"***Marriage Can Be Murder*** is hilarious, largely due to author Susan Santangelo's masterly description of what life is like as a baby boomer. Since this is the third book in the series, readers have much to enjoy."

–*Readers' Favorite*

"***Marriage Can Be Murder***, the third Baby Boomer mystery, is a wonderful extended family affair as even canines Lucy and Ethel help in the investigation. The inquiry is fun as Susan Santangelo provides an engaging amateur sleuth."

–*Midwest Book Review*

Class Reunions *Can Be* Murder

Every Wife Has A Story

A Carol and Jim Andrews Baby Boomer Mystery

Fourth in the Series

Susan Santangelo

Class Reunions Can Be Murder
A Baby Boomer Mysteries Press Book

PUBLISHING HISTORY
Baby Boomer Mysteries trade paperback edition/First Printing, June 2013

PUBLISHED BY
Baby Boomer Mysteries Press
P.O. Box 1491, West Dennis, MA
www.babyboomermysteries.com

This is a work of fiction. Names, characters, places and incidents are either the product of the author's imagination or used fictitiously.

Cover and Book Design by Grouper Design, Yarmouthport, MA.

Cover Art: Elizabeth Moisan

ISBN 978-0-9857799-1-7

Publisher's Note: The recipes in this book are to be followed exactly as written. The publisher and the author are not responsible for a reader's specific health or allergy needs which may require medical supervision. The publisher and the author are not responsible for any adverse reactions to the recipes contained in this book.

This book is dedicated to all the usual suspects:

Dave, Mark, Sandy, Rebecca, and Jacob. And especially to Joe, who supports and inspires me every day.

To all my high school classmates, who bear no resemblance whatsoever to any character in this book, thanks for the memories. And, especially, for the love and laughter.

A big shout out to Lynn Pray, Courtney Cherico, and Pineridge English Cockers, for adding our boy, Boomer, to our pack. And, Boomer, thanks for being such a handsome cover model. Sorry that you had to pose as two females, though.

Thanks to Elizabeth Moisan for the terrific cover art, and Kimberly White from Grouper Design for the book design. And for letting me add her sweet Labrador Retriever, Porter, to this storyline. Porter crossed the Rainbow Bridge last year with our wonderful old dog, Tucker. There will always be a place in my heart for both of them.

Thank you so much to Paulette DiAngi for the creative and delicious reunion recipes, found in the back of this book.

To everyone at the Breast Cancer Survival Center, and breast cancer survivors everywhere, God bless! And to those who are continuing to fight the fight, never give up!

A big thank you to everyone from the Cape Cod Hospital Auxiliary, Barnstable branch, and the Cape Cod Hospital Thrift Shop, for allowing me to play with them. Which I do as often as I can.

Thank you to Ryan Carr, Dennis MA Police Department, for patiently answering my questions.

For Carole Goldberg from *The Hartford Courant,* and Melanie Lauwers from the *Cape Cod Times,* I appreciate your help more than you will ever know.

To my own First Readers Club, I couldn't do this without your input. And Faith Scherer, thanks for the chapter heading!

To all my friends and cyber friends from Sisters in Crime, especially the New England chapter, thanks for sharing your expertise with me. I always learn something new, and the support is fantastic.

Thank you to the late Terri Ann Armstrong, my number one cheerleader, for her support. And to Shannon Raab, who helps me in so many ways.

And to everyone who's enjoyed this series – the readers I've met at countless book events and those who have e-mailed me – thanks so much! Hope you enjoy this one, too.

Fairport Manor Senior Living Community/a.k.a. Mount Saint Francis Academy

The Night Before The Reunion

"I don't know how I let you talk me into this," I said, huffing as I pulled my overnight bag up the marble stairs toward our third floor bedroom.

"Well, Carol," said my very best friend Nancy, "if you weren't such a nutcase about taking the elevator, we'd be in our room by now. I bet Claire and Mary Alice are already unpacked, lounging in their pajamas, and sipping a glass of cold chardonnay. While we're pulling suitcases up these damn stairs. And probably overstressing our hearts. Which could lead to a stroke. And death. Not the way I pictured spending our fortieth high school reunion."

I stopped in mid-stair and turned around to glare at Nancy. "It was your idea to stay here the night before the reunion lunch, in case you've forgotten," I said. "I only agreed to this after you badgered me for a week. There's absolutely no reason why we have to be here the night before. Even if we are running this event.

"Besides, I think it's creepy, being here in a practically empty building that used to be our high school. And that's going to open as a senior living facility in less than a week."

I pulled my suitcase up behind me, being careful not to slip on the stairs. The same stairs that I had maneuvered with such agility to get to class on time all those years ago. "It's more than creepy. It's weird."

"You're weird," Nancy shot back. "Let's go, already."

I bit back a sharp reply. Maybe I was weird. I've always been afraid of small spaces. Especially after I worked in New York City after college and got stuck in an elevator during one of the famous blackouts. For more hours than I cared to remember.

"We're here," announced Nancy. "Third floor, former cloister, and our home-away-from-home for tonight. And maybe tomorrow night, too."

No way was I going to stay here more than one night. But I decided to fight that battle in the morning. Or maybe I'd just slink away after the reunion lunch and let Nancy figure it out for herself.

"Are Claire and Mary Alice right next door to us?" I asked Nancy, forcing myself to look on the bright side. "We always have much more fun when the four of us are together."

Nancy frowned and looked at the key tag she had in her hand. "We're in three-one-eight. I think they're down at the end of the hall."

She paused and clutched her chest dramatically. "Gracious me, that climb was too much. I need to catch my breath. "

"If you're trying to make me feel guilty about our taking the stairs, forget it," I said, grabbing the key. "I happen to know that you have a much more strenuous daily exercise routine at the local torture chamber you call a women's fitness center. Climbing three flights of stairs should be a breeze for you."

I started to insert the key in the lock and the door immediately swung open. Without any help from me.

"That's funny," I said. "Why would our room be unlocked?"

"Maybe Goldilocks climbed in through the window and is waiting to share her porridge with us," Nancy said.

"Very funny," I said, going into our bedroom first and fumbling for the wall light switch.

"Oh." I stopped so quickly that Nancy bumped into me.

Someone was sleeping in one of the beds. A quick glance revealed it was a woman with short white hair.

"Excuse me," I said in my most take-charge voice. "I'm sorry to wake you, but you're in the wrong room."

"We all make mistakes as we get a little older," Nancy said. "But she sure is a sound sleeper. She didn't even stir when we came in."

I leaned down and touched the woman's right arm, which was peeking out of the bedclothes. Nothing. No response.

"Nancy," I said as my stomach began to do unexpected flip-flops, "let's get out of here. Now. I hope you have your phone with you."

"I always have my phone with me," Nancy said. "But who on earth do you want to call at this hour of the night?"

"The Fairport police," I said, trying to remain calm even though I wanted to run up and down the hall, shrieking my head off. "Whoever this woman is, she's not sleeping.

"She's dead."

Chapter 1

Mrs. Brown, you've got a lovely walker.

"Close your eyes, Carol," said my BFF Nancy. "I can't wait to show you what I found yesterday when I was cleaning out a closet."

I leaned back in my kitchen chair and closed my eyes obediently, willing my mouth to refrain from the snappy comment that had sprung, unbidden, into my mind. *If my eyes are closed, how can I see what you have to show me?*

"You can open them now, Carol," Nancy said. "Ta dah!"

I couldn't believe my eyes. "Is that our old high school blazer you're wearing?" I asked. "Good lord, where did you find that relic?"

"I told you, Carol, I found it when I was cleaning out a closet. I wanted to put together a bag of donations for Sally's Closet. The thrift shop supports such a good cause, helping victims of domestic abuse. I know the shop always needs donations of gently worn women's clothing.

"One of my New Year's resolutions was getting rid of things I don't really need or will never use again. Like my husband, for instance."

I turned my gaze away from the navy blue blazer with the insignia of Mount Saint Francis Academy emblazoned on the breast pocket to stare at my best friend. "Are you trying to tell me something, Nancy? Have you really decided to divorce Bob?"

"Nah," Nancy said. "Not so far, anyway. I'm having too much fun dating him. It's much better than living with Bob fulltime and having to pick up his dirty socks off the bathroom floor and cook his meals. Now that we're living separately, we're getting along great. And before you ask me the next question on your mind, I'm not the least bit worried that he'll cheat on me again. Because I already warned him that if he does, I'll turn the tables and start dating, too. My Dream Dates profile is still active, and I get e-mails about potential dates every week. I make sure I let good old Bob know that."

She twirled in front of me so I could admire her again. "I hope you've noticed that I can still button this blazer, Carol. And I'm not even holding my breath. "

"I noticed," I said. "I'm impressed. And jealous, too. Although I have no desire to put on my navy blue blazer ever again. I was so thrilled to finally get out of that place that I remember doing a cartwheel on the lawn after graduation. Unfortunately, I was wearing shorts under my graduation robe, not the required white graduation dress. And Sister Rose caught me.'

I grimaced at the memory. "She was pretty good at that."

"I saw Sister Rose this morning when I brought my donations to the shop," Nancy said.

I immediately stiffened. Mention of our former high school English teacher still made me do that.

"She mentioned you hadn't been in to volunteer at the thrift shop for several months," Nancy went on. "I told her you'd been very busy with Jenny and Mark's wedding."

A minor understatement. I'd been busy with the wedding, but even busier clearing Nancy's cheating husband from suspicion in the death of our wedding planner.

You remember that, right?

I was sure Nancy did, so I didn't bring it up and make her relive the nightmare all over again. Good friend that I am.

"I told Sister Rose that I'd found my old Mount Saint Francis blazer. We had a good laugh about it. You know, Carol, it's been almost forty years since we graduated."

"Don't remind me," I said. "Next you'll be figuring out how long it's been since we got out of grammar school."

"What do you think about Claire, Mary Alice, you and me getting together for a reunion lunch?" Nancy said. "For old times' sake."

"A reunion lunch? What are you talking about, Nancy? The four of us get together for lunch at least twice a month. I suppose you could call them 'reunion lunches,' since we all went to school together. But I just think of them as lunches with my three best friends in the world."

"Actually," Nancy said, "I was thinking it might be nice to add a few more people to a lunch sometime later this year. Just for the heck of it. What do you think? Aren't there a few people from our high school class that you'd like to see again?"

I thought for minute, came up empty, and shook my head.

"I can't think of a single person."

"Oh, come on, Carol. Don't kid me. How about Cynthia Perkins? You and she used to be great pals. I remember she even fixed you up with her brother for one of our fall formals."

"That didn't go well," I reminded Nancy. "The cheapskate didn't even buy me a corsage."

"Well, you can't hold Cynthia responsible if her brother turned out to be a jerk," Nancy said. "What about Joanne Mitchell. She was a real brainiac. Don't you wonder what ever happened to her?"

I shook my head. "Nope, can't say I've given her a single thought in forty years."

"But that's exactly my point, Carol," Nancy said, not willing to let the subject go. "It's forty years. That's a heck of a long time. I think we need to celebrate. All of us. Well, as many people as we can find from our class. At a reunion lunch at Mount Saint Francis.

"Before it's turned into a senior living facility."

Chapter 2

I lost my temper twenty years ago and haven't found it yet.

"Well, you've succeeded in capturing my attention," I said, opening the kitchen door and letting Lucy and Ethel, our two English cocker spaniels, back into the house after a romp in the yard. I tossed each dog a treat, then continued, "Tell me what you know about Mount Saint Francis. And who's your source for this rumor? I don't remember reading anything about this in the local paper."

Nancy started to answer, but I stopped her. "Let me make a fresh pot of coffee. I have a feeling this is going to call for lots of caffeine." I pulled out a kitchen chair and gestured her to sit. "And for Pete's sake, take that blazer off. You're giving me the willies."

"It's not a rumor, Carol. It's a fact. I heard it today from Sister Rose. And she's hardly one to spread unfounded gossip."

"True," I agreed. "I'm sure all the gossip she spreads is founded in absolute fact."

"Carol, how can you say that? She runs a domestic violence crisis center, for heaven's sake. If anyone believes in confidentiality, it's Sister Rose."

I set two mugs of steaming coffee on the kitchen table. Black, in case you were wondering. I've decided it's way past the time to shed those extra pounds around my middle, and giving up sugar is an easy way to start. At least, that's what I tell myself.

"All right, already. You're right, Nancy. I take back my remark about Sister Rose. It was unfair and completely untrue. Now, tell me what's going on with Mount Saint Francis."

"The volunteer in the back of the shop insisted on checking over my donation, to be sure there wasn't anything ripped or stained," Nancy huffed, veering completely off the subject. "As if I'd ever do something like that! Then, the shop has this whole long paperwork thingie that had to be filled out. Name, address, phone, and estimated value of the donation. That last part was tough. I gave them two cashmere sweaters that I'd barely worn, a Calvin Klein suit, four pairs of Ralph Lauren pants, and a beautiful black leather purse. I had a lot of trouble figuring out what to put down, but Sister Rose told me that if I put down more than five hundred dollars, I had to have receipts to justify the amount in case I was ever audited by the IRS. So I put down five hundred dollars."

I rolled my eyes. And waited. I knew Nancy would get to the point. Eventually.

"Once that was out of the way, Sister Rose spent at least fifteen minutes giving me an earful about what was going on at Mount Saint Francis. You know that it's been a conference center for the last ten years, right?"

I nodded. "I've seen ads for it in the local paper. It would creep me out to go to a conference there, though. I just can't imagine going back."

"Sister Rose told me that, even though the conference center has been run by an outside company, the nuns still own the property," Nancy said. "But the outside company wasn't able to host enough conferences to make a profit. So when their lease expired, the company didn't renew it. The good sisters were pretty upset. I mean, let's face it, the place really is a white elephant."

"True," I said, finally getting a word in. "But even if the building itself isn't worth much, I bet the land it's standing on is. Views of Long Island Sound always hike up property values in Fairfield County."

"I know that, Carol," said my friend Nancy the Realtor, giving me a disgusted look. "You don't have to tell me."

"Sorry, Nancy. Of course you know that. I was just reminding you."

Nancy patted my hand. "I kind of overreacted there. I just don't like anyone suggesting I don't know how to do my job."

Sheesh.

"Anyway," Nancy continued, "as luck would have it, Dockside Living, the big Connecticut senior living conglomerate, was looking for something in Fairfield County. The nuns are going to lease the property to them, and they're getting some nice money from the deal. Much more than they got from the conference center company. The plan is to turn our school into an active adult community with an assisted living component. The permits have gone through without a hitch, so the renovations will begin immediately. Don't you think that's great?"

"I'm not sure that 'great' is exactly the word I'd choose," I said. "But I can see why the nuns agreed. I hope you didn't sign us up for a unit." I narrowed my eyes. "Or, more to the point, hustled Sister Rose into giving you the exclusive right to be the listing agent for the place."

"I didn't think of that," Nancy said. "What a great idea. After all, I am the best Realtor in Fairport. I'll have to suggest that to Sister the next time I see her."

She whipped out her smartphone and made a quick note.

"Anyway, Sister Rose had a really terrific idea," Nancy went on. "The renovations to the building are supposed to take about five months. Dockside Living would like to do some sort of grand opening event, marketing to an appropriate age bracket.

"Sister Rose suggested the event be our fortieth class reunion. And for you and me to organize it."

Chapter 3

There is nothing more boring than looking at someone else's yearbook.

I carefully put my coffee cup down, then blotted my lips with a napkin and prayed for inner peace. And the right words to nix this nutty idea right now.

"Of course, you said no to Sister, Nancy. You did, didn't you?"

I looked closely at her face. Guilt was written all over it. In capital letters.

"Are you out of your mind?" I sputtered. "I hate the very idea of *going* to a class reunion. No way am I helping to organize one. Forget it."

Nancy sighed deeply. "I knew this would be your first reaction. But I'm sure that, when you give the reunion some thought, you'll decide that it's going to be loads of fun. And we'll get Mary Alice and Claire involved, too. It'll be great!" Her eyes sparkled at the very thought.

Yuck.

"There is absolutely no way I'm going to do it, Nancy," I said again, "so save your breath. You know that I haven't gone to any of our high school reunions. And I never want to. Ever. So why the heck would I agree to help organize our fortieth?"

I paused for emphasis, then leveled my very best friend from pre-puberty days with the most chilling glare I could come up with. And believe me, I had plenty of glares to choose from. Practice makes perfect, and all that stuff. After more than thirty-five years of marriage to Jim, and raising two children – who were almost perfect but not quite – I'd had plenty of practice.

Nancy opened her mouth to respond, then thought better of it. Instead, she matched my glare with one of her own. I could almost hear the wheels in her brain clicking, as she searched for the perfect rebuttal for my argument.

But I'd been on the debate team at Mount Saint Francis Academy, too. I was confident that whatever she came up with, I could refute. And thereby end the conversation.

"How can you disappoint Sister Rose and all the other sisters who are counting on this facility to give the order a much-needed shot of cash? So even more victims of domestic abuse can be helped at Sally's Place. You know how important that program is. Those poor people flee from an abusive situation with absolutely nothing. And they need the help that Sally's Place gives them. How can you say no?"

"You know I want to help Sally's Place," I said, ignoring Nancy's questionable leap of logic. "But this reunion idea is nuts."

The more I thought about the reunion, the more I was convinced that the idea hadn't come from our teacher at all.

"Is this really something Sister Rose suggested, or did you give her the idea?" I eyed my very best friend and she looked away without giving me an answer.

"Why didn't she just ask me herself?" I continued. "And why would she have anything to say about it, anyway? It's our class, after all. Is she still trying to call the shots after all these years?"

"Well," Nancy admitted after a lengthy pause, "maybe I mentioned the reunion to Sister Rose first. And asked her for some input. After all, she was our English teacher for junior and senior years. And she's the only nun from school who we ever see."

"Whom," I said.

Nancy looked at me and raised one eyebrow. I hate people who can do that. I've tried for years to master that technique but always look like I have an uncontrollable twitch.

"Sister Rose is the only nun from school *whom* we ever see. Whom is the direct object of the verb in that sentence."

"Yeah, right. Whatever you say, Carol," Nancy said.

"Moving on, when I mentioned that our class graduated from Mount Saint Francis forty years ago, Sister Rose wanted to know what we were planning to mark the occasion. I didn't know what to say, since nobody had talked about a reunion."

"Exactly," I said. "Because nothing is planned."

"Well, you remember how persuasive Sister Rose can be," Nancy said.

"I remember how intimidating she can be," I countered. "That's not exactly the same thing. But close enough, I guess."

"Ok, Carol. I admit that the reunion was mostly my idea. But Sister loved it."

"I thought so. And whose idea was it to get me involved? Tell the truth, Nancy."

"Well," Nancy said, coming clean at last, "I guess it was mine. But Sister immediately agreed with me. I mean, Carol, you're the best party planner I know. Your neighborhood Bunco parties are the stuff of legend. And your holiday open house, well, everyone who's anyone in Fairport wants to be on your guest list."

"Flattery will get you nowhere, Nancy," I said. But it was true, I'm a good organizer. And my parties are, well, fun. I just had no desire to use my party-planning skills to organize my high school reunion.

Unless, of course, I could organize the whole darn thing and then not go.

Chapter 4

Shake it up, baby! Twist and shout!
Oh, damn, I threw my back out!

"I think a high school reunion sounds like a blast," said my darling daughter Jenny, turning to her brand new husband, Fairport police detective Mark Anderson, for his opinion. "Wouldn't it be great to get some of our old gang together again?"

"That's because your old gang isn't as old as your mother's," my own husband reminded Jenny.

"Watch what you say, buster," I said to Jim, shaking my fork at him. "Your old gang and mine are the same vintage."

"Oh, these family suppers," Jenny said, laughing. "Another chance to watch Mom and Dad try to one-up each other. It's sort of like watching one of those political talk shows with a liberal pundit trying to outshout a conservative one. And each trying to convince the other one that he's right."

"But we do it with love," I said, smarting slightly from the implied criticism. "That's the difference."

"Of course you do, Mom," said Jenny. "And if you don't want to be involved in your high school reunion, that's your business."

"Exactly right," I said, beaming at her.

"Still," she said, not wanting to let the subject drop, "you'd do such a great job organizing it. And I bet it would be fun. Just think of all the old friends you could find."

"People I haven't thought about in years are hardly what I'd call old friends, Jenny. And no cracks about 'old,' Jim. I'm exactly one month younger than you are."

So far, Mark had remained quiet during the Andrews family entertainment hour. But he couldn't resist adding a comment.

"You know, Carol, you could be smart skipping all your reunions. I've been hearing some stories down at police headquarters that are downright scary. About people who've been holding a childhood grudge for years, and then, bam, they go to a class reunion and all the old hurts and insecurities come back."

"Who'd harbor a grudge for all those years?" Jim asked. "Nobody I know."

"Then you're lucky, Jim," Mark said. "As a matter of fact, there was an instance a few months ago about some guy who always felt he'd been blackballed from the high school football team by another classmate. He tracked the classmate down through the high school reunion committee, went to his door and rang the bell. When the poor sap answered, he took a shot at him. Fortunately, the shooter had lousy aim and hit the doorframe, not the intended victim. But he was still arrested. And the victim didn't even remember who the shooter was."

I was so shocked by Mark's story that I almost dropped the basket of rolls I was passing around the table.

"I doubt that anyone from my class at Mount Saint Francis Academy is holding that kind of a grudge, Mark. That's ridiculous."

"Oh, I don't know about that, Carol," Jim said. "I've heard you, Nancy, Claire and Mary Alice swap stories about girls who stole other girls' boyfriends. Not that any of you did, of course."

I was speechless. But not for long. I'm sure all of you who've known me for a while aren't surprised by that.

"I don't know what you're talking about, *dear*," I shot back. "And, by the way, maybe you shouldn't eavesdrop on private conversations that don't concern you."

And, as far as I was concerned, that was the end of our discussion about my high school days. And a possible high school reunion.

But to be absolutely sure that my well-meaning, and nosy, family wouldn't gang up on me again, I immediately switched the subject of our conversation to Jim's favorite subject – local politics. In no time at all, he and Mark were deeply embroiled in the merits of the police department's request to add six more patrolman to the roster. Which would mean safer streets and better service and more protection for the citizens of Fairport (Mark), and a hefty increase in the police budget to pay for the additional personnel, which the town couldn't afford (Jim).

Am I good or what?

Chapter 5

I used to be indecisive. But now, I'm not sure.

I knew Monday was going to be a bad day as soon as I stumbled into the kitchen. It was empty.

Oh, Lucy and Ethel were there, curled up together in a weak patch of sunlight. Sorry if I misled you.

But apparently Jim had left the house early in the morning, and I didn't hear him. Ohmygod. I was always accusing him of losing his hearing. Maybe I was losing mine, too. Or my mind.

Nah, that went bye-bye a while ago, to hear my family tell it.

And there was no coffee made. Rats. Jim always made the morning coffee. It was one of the few perks (pun intended) of his being retired. I'd become accustomed to coming down to breakfast and being able to pour myself a cup of caffeine right away. Plus, he made it better than I did. I don't know how – he just did.

No coffee. And no "I've gone, and I'll be back, and have a good day" love note, either.

Double rats. But it looked like Jim had walked and fed both dogs, from the two dirty dog bowls in the sink and the open bag of kibble on the granite countertop.

"You drink far too much coffee, anyway," I told myself. "How about starting the day with a nice cup of Earl Grey tea for a change?"

Feeling extra virtuous, I reached for the tea kettle just as the phone rang. Caller ID told me it was Claire.

I checked the time on the stove – it was barely 8:30 a.m.

"I guess Larry is up and out early too, Claire," I said by way of greeting. "Good early morning to you."

"I called to tell you that you're being a real jerk," said my former good friend. "I think it will be lots of fun to go check out our old high school. None of us are signing a lease to live there. Sister Rose really wants us to see it before the major construction work begins. Mary Alice and Nancy refuse to go if you won't come with us."

Say what?

I was shocked. This really hit me hard. Claire and I have been close friends since way before puberty. Heck, we were close before either of us understood what puberty was.

Claire has always been the ultrasmart one in our group. All A's, without really trying. Well, maybe she pulled a few all-nighters now and then, but good grades – great grades – mega good grades – just seemed to happen to her.

Nancy was the pretty one in our group. Mary Alice was the sweet one. As for me, well, maybe I was the comic relief. Or the mouthy one. You pick. My feelings won't be hurt. Much.

Back in the day (and I'm not saying what "day" I'm referring to), grammar school teachers used to seat their students in alphabetical order by last name. So when I started first grade at Mount Saint Francis Grammar School in Fairport, Connecticut, I was placed next to a cute, dark-haired girl named Nancy Kendrick. I was Carol Kerr then, in case you didn't know that. (Or Carol Elizabeth Kerr, as my mother referred to me when I was in trouble.) Nancy and I became best friends instantly, and it helped that the Kendricks lived two blocks from our house. Those were the days when children could walk to school unsupervised, and safely play outside for hours. We even got our first bikes the same day.

Nancy and I were inseparable from first through third grade. And then a new family moved in next door to the Kendricks. The Bennetts. And they had a little girl, too. Mary Alice. The Bennetts enrolled Mary Alice in Mount Saint Francis Grammar School, too.

Nancy and Mary Alice became fast friends. And began walking to school together. Leaving me out of their new, tight friendship. At least, that's how it seemed to me. Boy, was I hurt.

Most of fourth grade was terrible for me. Until another new girl transferred into our class in the middle of the year – Claire Monahan. And I befriended her.

Somehow, over that summer between fourth and fifth grade, the four of us became a group. I don't remember the details. But we all just clicked, and the old hurts (on my part) were put aside.

Thank God.

I know how special it is to make friends in grammar school, strengthen the friendship bonds in high school and college and be even closer now that we're all adults. We've shared just about everything with each other over the years – broken hearts, broken bones, weddings, funerals, children's births, the death of a spouse. And lots of laughter and love.

Sometimes I think that Nancy, Claire and Mary Alice understand me better – and know more about me – than my own family. Except Lucy and Ethel, of course.

But as long as I'm being honest with you, I'll admit that, for some reason, Claire is the only member of our foursome who intimidates me. I say that in a loving way. But she's always been…perfect. Even when she gained some weight in her fifties. She's very tall, so she carried the extra pounds like an Amazon goddess. (Not that she saw herself that way, of course.)

And when Claire's hair turned white, every strand was gorgeous. Not that she thought so. That's why she went through a brief stage as a redhead. Maybe some of you remember that.

Anyway, what I'm trying to say is that Claire can intimidate me. It's not that I don't love her as much as my other best friends. But, everything she does, she does brilliantly.

Oh, well.

I resisted the urge to bang the phone down in her ear. My mother raised me to be polite. But this was not the way I wanted my Monday to start.

"Nobody mentioned a trip to check out the school," I said, searching my rusty memory bank to be sure I was correct. "Nancy was trying to strong-arm me into helping her organize our class reunion. Which I absolutely refused to do."

Silence from the other end of the line.

"As far as visiting Mount Saint Francis, I never said I wouldn't do that. I haven't had the urge to go back… well … ever. Not since we all graduated. But I'll think about it," I said. "This is the first time anyone's bothered to mention this idea to me."

Considering that I was caffeine-deprived, I felt that was a major concession on my part.

"Great," said Claire. "Be ready at eleven-thirty."

"Today?" I said. "You mean, we're going today?"

"No time like the present," Claire said. "I'll pick you up at eleven-thirty sharp. I told Nancy that I'd have much better luck talking you into this than she or Mary Alice would. And I was right! See you later." She clicked off.

"I've been had, Lucy," I said, directing my comment to the dominant English cocker in the house. "I bet you knew about this all the time and didn't have the decency to warn me. And you probably hid all the coffee, too. Just to weaken me."

Lucy gave me a reproachful stare, telegraphing as clear as anything that neither she nor Ethel would stoop so low. Especially because she knew that if she hid the coffee, I'd retaliate by hiding the dog biscuits. Swear to God, that's what she said.

Chapter 6

I wanna hold your hand. If I don't, I might fall down.

"This is going to be so much fun," Claire said. She gave me a quick glance to see if I agreed with her Pollyanna description of our upcoming adventure.

"It's a nice day for a ride," I said, choosing to ignore the point of her remark. "And I'm glad you're driving, not me. It's good to be a passenger for a change. I love your new car."

"I always wanted a red convertible. And I figured, there's no time like the present, right? We're not getting any younger."

"The truth hurts," I said. "But coming from someone who's my own age, it doesn't hurt nearly as much. Don't you just hate it when some smart-alecky twenty-something calls you ma'am? It makes me feel like somebody's grandmother."

"I thought becoming a grandmother was your next career goal, Carol," Claire said. "Especially now that you've finally managed to get Jenny and Mark married."

"From your mouth to God's ears, Claire," I said with a laugh. "But this is one project that I can't organize. Oversee. Control. You can pick whatever word you want."

I sighed. "I just hope they don't wait too long before they decide to have a baby. They're both so wrapped up in their careers."

"Like that's such a bad thing?" Claire questioned. "Mark's been promoted to detective in the Fairport Police Department. And Jenny's finally gotten her master's degree and is well on her way to her Ph.D. in

English. She's a natural teacher, and Fairport College is thrilled to have her as an adjunct. You should be proud of both of them."

"I am proud of both of them," I said in my own defense. "Very proud. But this generation seems to be prone to getting all wrapped up in their careers and putting off starting a family until the woman is in her forties. And then there can be all sorts of problems conceiving. I don't want that to happen to Jenny and Mark."

Claire took her right hand off the steering wheel, just for a second, and gave me a slap. It was a gentle slap. But a slap nonetheless.

"Carol, knock it off. For heaven's sake, they've only been married a few months. Stop imagining problems where they don't exist. You really are too much."

"I guess you're right," I said, trying my best to sound convinced that Claire's theory about me was correct. Oh, heck, I knew Claire was right. But that didn't mean I'd let the subject drop without one parting shot.

Except, for once in my life, I couldn't think of one. How about that? Well, there is a first time for everything.

"It looks like the street has been widened," I said as we drove up Hilltop Avenue toward the school. "The last time I was here…uh, oh…"

Claire swiveled her head toward me so fast I was afraid it was going to snap off her neck.

"What do you mean, 'the last time you were here,' Carol?" she asked. "Have you been up here recently? You swore to us that you never came back to Mount Saint Francis after we graduated."

"Keep your eyes on the road, Claire," I said. "And you misunderstood what I said just now."

"Oh, yeah, right," said Claire. "How come I don't believe you?"

Rats. I was trapped. And by my own big mouth, too.

We turned into the driveway leading to our school. Claire pulled over to the side and killed the car engine. "We're not going anywhere until you level with me," she said.

"It's really no big deal," I said.

"It's a big deal because you've made it one for forty years," Claire said. "You said you'd never come back to school again after graduation. And every time the three of us tried to entice you into coming to an event to benefit Mount Saint Francis, you flatly refused to go.

"So, what gives?"

I thought fast.

"I discovered a while back that Hilltop Avenue is a handy short-cut to get to the beach if the main roads are clogged," I said. "I use it when the tourists are around. You know how Fairport gets invaded with all those summer people. That's the whole story. Honest."

"And you want me to believe that not once, in one of your short-cut adventures, you never had the urge to drive in and check out Mount Saint Francis? With your nosy nature? Oh, puhleeze. No way am I going to swallow that one. I bet that, knowing you, you probably got out of your car and peeked in the windows."

"Ok, ok. I've been back here before," I said. "I admit it. I was curious about how the building looked after all these years. So sue me.

"But I did *not* peek in the windows. I swear."

"Why didn't you want any of us to know, Carol? I don't understand about the secrecy," Claire said.

"Well, I'd made such a big deal out of never coming back here again, I guess I was embarrassed to admit that I had. I didn't want everybody making fun of me."

"Honestly, Carol, none of us would have made fun of you. We'd want to know how the old place looked, of course. In as much detail as you could remember. But we wouldn't have razzed you for going back. After all, we had four great years here. Even if you have trouble admitting it."

Claire turned the key in the ignition and the motor leaped to life. "Just wait until I tell Nancy and Mary Alice about this."

"Claire, I'd rather you didn't," I said. "I'm not worried about Mary Alice's reaction, but Nancy will probably use it to strong-arm me into helping her organize our fortieth reunion. Which I really don't want to do. Will you keep my secret? For old times' sake?"

"You're a doofus, Carol," Claire said. "But I love you and, if that's what you want, I won't mention it." She turned the car into a parking space in front of the building.

"We're here. And I, for one, can't wait to see how our old high school is being transformed into a senior living facility. Grab your walker and let's go."

Ha! That Claire. What a kidder.

I may be a teeny bit prejudiced, but I have to admit that Mount Saint Francis Academy is one of the most impressive and beautiful structures I've ever seen. The building was originally a mansion owned by the Carny family, who could trace their lineage back to the founding fathers (and mothers) of Fairport. In fact, not only was one of their ancestors a hero in the American Revolution, George Washington really did sleep at his house. At least, that's what the family always claimed.

The building is brick with limestone trim, designed in the style of many of the mansions on Newport, Rhode Island's, famed Cliff Walk. Its imposing entrance topped by a curved portico is flanked by massive white marble pillars which have weathered to a dusty beige over the past century.

Elizabeth Carny, the last of the family line, was a great believer in education for "young ladies." A devout Catholic, she donated the mansion to the local order of nuns, stipulating in her will that the building be used primarily to educate and nurture young women.

Mount Saint Francis Academy educated thousands of young women since it opened its doors in the early 1900s. Including me and my three best friends. And here we were, back again. And still together.

"Where are Nancy and Mary Alice?" I asked, stalling for time before I went inside our high school after a forty-year year absence.

It felt weird to walk up the front steps and stand under the portico for the very first time. When we were students at Mount Saint Francis, we were never allowed to use the front entrance. That was reserved for very important guests, like the bishop. I remember that all the nuns were in a tizzy every time he came by.

Don't get me wrong – the bishop didn't just drop in unannounced. In fact, we always had at least a month's advance notice that he was coming. But that didn't lessen the nervous excitement that permeated the entire building when he was expected. In fact, it seemed to heighten it.

There was even a special parlor, directly adjacent to the main corridor, reserved just to greet His Nibs. When he wasn't around, the door was kept closed. I often wondered if anyone went in there to dust, or if there was cleaning frenzy just before his expected arrival.

I couldn't imagine what would have happened if the Pope popped in to say hi. Probably massive coronaries in the cloister.

"Maybe Mary Alice and Nancy left their cars in the back parking lot," Claire said. "Don't forget, there's another entrance off Shore Road. Where our parents used to drop us off for school, a thousand years ago."

"The place doesn't seem to have changed that much," I said. "At least, from the outside. I think adding two rocking chairs by the front door would be a nice touch. Or maybe two walkers would be better."

"Remember, the place isn't open yet," Claire said. "The management company is just beginning the transformation, so try not to be so critical."

I bit my tongue. I was just kidding, for heaven's sake. I am the least critical person I know. In fact, a critical word never escapes my lips. But if a critical thought…or two…or three…should happen to wander into my head, well, that's a whole different story.

"Do we knock?" I asked. "Or maybe we should just walk in."

I stepped aside and pushed Claire in front of me. "You go first. You're taller than I am."

Claire gave me a look of undisguised exasperation and reached for the front door. Only to have it fly open and reveal Nancy and Mary Alice, giggling like the school girls we used to be.

"We were watching you from the window in the parlor," Nancy said. "I bet Mary Alice ten dollars that Claire would never get you up the front steps, Carol. You actually made it, so I guess I have to treat you to lunch, Mary Alice."

"You can treat me to lunch, too, Nancy," I said, only slightly miffed at having my very best friend make fun of me. "And Claire, too, for that matter."

"It's odd to be back here after all these years," Mary Alice said, giving me a quick hug. "The place looks the same, but it feels different. That probably doesn't make any sense."

I looked around and nodded in agreement. "I think you've made perfect sense, Mary Alice. It's the same, but different. For instance, what happened to the statue of Saint Francis that used to be next to the door? Remember that?"

"I remember that one Halloween night we sneaked up the hill in the dark and put a lighted cigar in his hand," Nancy said. "Then we rang the front doorbell and ran away when one of the nuns came to answer it."

Claire looked shocked. "I don't remember that at all. You're making it up. I'm certain I was never part of that adventure. My God, you could have burned the whole place down. "

"Nancy and I were the ones who put the cigar in Saint Francis's hand," I said. "And Mary Alice rang the doorbell. You were the first one to get a driver's license, so you drove the getaway car, Claire. Whether you own up to it or not."

I paused for maximum effect. "But first, Nancy had to get the darn cigar to light. And since we were all non-smokers, that took some doing.

And lots of puffing." I mimed Nancy lighting the cigar, puffing on it, then doubling over, coughing.

That did it. We all shrieked with laughter as the memory of that long-ago night surfaced with such clarity in our late-middle-aged brains that it might have happened yesterday.

"Get a grip," Nancy said, trying to bring us under control. "We're supposed to be grown-ups now."

"Fat chance," I said, and we started hooting all over again. "Maybe we should organize a search party to find Saint Francis. I wonder if we can file a missing statue report with the Fairport police. Is that the same as a missing person's report? Can we be considered next-of-kin because we're graduates of Mount Saint Francis?"

"Carol, you are too much," said Mary Alice.

"Thank you. I think."

I looked around what appeared to be a deserted lobby. "I hope nobody overheard us."

"Relax, Carol. I think the statute of limitations has expired," Nancy said. "Or maybe I should call it the 'statue' of limitations. At least we have an in with a good lawyer. Assuming Claire will put in a good word for us with Larry."

I rolled my eyes, and Mary Alice said, "I'm not the least bit worried."

"Of course you're not," Nancy said. "Ringing the doorbell on Halloween night was probably the only thing you ever did wrong in the whole four years we were in high school."

Now it was Mary Alice's turn to roll her eyes. "If that's what you think, I'm not saying another word. Or confessing anything else. I have secrets, too."

Hmm. This was turning into a pretty surprising day.

"Where's the person from the management company who's supposed to show us around?" Claire asked. "I thought we had an appointment."

"We're waiting for Sister Rose to get here," Nancy said.

I had my usual knee-jerk reaction. Emphasis on the word "jerk."

"You didn't tell me Sister Rose was going to be part of our tour group."

"I thought you and she were best buddies now, Carol," Claire said. "Especially after you loaned your house for her to use as a fundraiser for Sally's Place. I know that party raised big bucks for the domestic violence victims program."

"And let's not forget about your volunteer gig at Sally's Closet," Nancy said. "Although your motives for being there may not be exactly pure. I know what a great shopping opportunity it is for you, to be able to scoop up some great bargains before they even hit the sales floor."

"How does that old saying go, Nancy? Something about the pot calling the kettle black when the pot is black, too? Do I have that right?" I shot back, eager to be off the hot seat.

"You know," I said, looking around what used to be the formal entrance to our old high school, "being back here again makes me feel like I'm still fifteen years old, and about to be called to the office because I was late for class. Or my pleated skirt was too short."

"Or your saddle shoes weren't shined," added Mary Alice. "I know exactly what you mean. I'm feeling the same way myself."

"Maybe that's why I reacted the way I did when I heard that Sister Rose was joining our group today. I guess, because we're back at school, it's like she's still the English teacher who used to strike fear into my heart every time I went into her classroom," I said. "But she can't scare me anymore."

I heard someone cough. Right behind me.

"She's here, isn't she?" I whispered to Claire, who nodded, then bypassed me to envelope our former teacher in a hug. Immediately followed by Nancy and Mary Alice.

I hung back, mindful of the fact that I had been AWOL from my regular volunteer stint (and, yes, shopping opportunity) at the thrift shop since way before Christmas. And nervous about being reprimanded by The Good Sister, just like in The Bad Old Days.

Old habits die hard. Pun intended.

Chapter 7

Bruce Springsteen was born to run. I was born to ride in a chauffeur-driven limousine.

In case any of you were wondering, Sister Rose looked as terrific as ever. Her face bore no age lines, which I assumed was nature being kind to her. (As far as I know, nuns can't have Botox treatments.) Her salt and pepper hair was short, cut in a no-nonsense style which was very becoming. And her two-piece gray pantsuit flattered a still slim figure.

"That's a great outfit, Sister," Claire said. "I bet I know where you got it."

Sister Rose laughed. "I shop in the most unique boutique in Fairport," she said, then flashed me a bright smile and – gasp – a wink. Which I chose to mean that I was forgiven for being absent from the shop, but I better show up soon to work.

Very soon.

I matched Sister Rose's smile with one of my own. (I did refuse to wink back, though. I am not a total suck-up.)

"Hello, Sister," I said. "It's nice to see you again. And I know I haven't been in to help at Sally's Closet for a long time. Life has been pretty hectic for me the last few months."

I shot Nancy a look, telegraphing, *Help me out here. Before I say something stupid.*

Best friend that she is, Nancy picked up on my message and immediately switched subjects. "How does it feel for you to be back at Mount Saint Francis after all these years?" she asked Sister Rose. "But

I suppose you've been here many times, since the sisters still own the property."

"For all of us, though," Claire added, "it's like being back in high school, waiting for the bell to ring for our next class."

Sister Rose laughed. "I know what you mean, Claire. Every time I come back here, I get that same peculiar feeling. But I'm sure that, as the renovation work continues, the building will look less like Mount Saint Francis and more like a senior living community. It's really going to be gorgeous when it's completed."

"There doesn't seem to be anyone around," Mary Alice said. "We're getting a tour of the facility, aren't we?"

"J.T. promised to be finished with another appointment by two-thirty," Sister Rose said, checking her wristwatch. "I said I was on a very tight schedule today." She looked at us apologetically. "I have a meeting with a potential donor to Sally's Place at three-thirty. I can't risk keeping her waiting. Did any of you walk around the first floor to see if J.T. was here?"

I resisted telling Sister Rose that none of us knew who J.T. was, or even if the person was male or female. But it was hard. Smart-alecky remarks are all too often my sentences of choice.

"Who's J.T.?" asked Mary Alice. "Forgive me if I'm supposed to know the answer, Sister."

"This isn't a pop quiz, so relax, Mary Alice," Sister Rose said. "J.T. is the marketing director for the new facility. It's her job to show the units to prospective residents. And one of the ways she's supposed to do that is by being available to take people on tours and point out how wonderful this place is going to be when it's completed."

Sister Rose's pursed her lips together in a tight line, and I was glad I wasn't in J.T.'s shoes.

"I think I hear voices from the lower level," Claire said.

"Let's go see," said Nancy. "I remember the old cafeteria was downstairs."

We had just started toward the stairs when the voices got louder. And louder. Two voices, a strident male one and a screeching female one.

Arguing.

Since I automatically shrink from confrontation of any kind, even if it doesn't involve me, I backed away from the stairs. Not Sister Rose, though.

"J.T., is that you?" she called out. "What is going on downstairs? Kindly remember that you are supposed to be giving a tour to four alumnae of Mount Saint Francis Academy. And myself. And that these are the same four alumnae who will be planning a reunion event to officially open this facility. You're certainly not making a very good impression."

A woman in her late thirties appeared at the top of the stairs. Her face was as bright red as her hair. Yelling can do that to a person – turn their face, red, I mean. Don't ask me how I know that. I just do.

"I'm terribly sorry to keep all of you waiting," she said. "And for having you overhear that...discussion with our new food service manager. Who is very displeased with the size of the kitchen. I told him this was the standard size for all of our facilities, and he'd better get used to it if he wanted to work here. Period."

J.T.'s posture gave no doubt as to which person has come out on top in that "discussion." Clearly, this was someone who was used to calling the shots.

She took a deep breath to calm herself, then addressed herself to Sister Rose. "I'm the only member of the management team here today, so I'm the construction foreman, too, I guess. But don't worry, Sister. Everything will be ironed out. There are always a few bumpy spots when Dockside Living is opening a new facility."

Sister Rose gave the woman a quick nod. Which was about as far as she was prepared to go, under the circumstances. All was not forgiven. If there was one thing Sister couldn't stand, it was to be kept waiting. For anything.

Like homework assignments, for instance.

Don't ask me how I know this, either. Let's just say that my long-term memory is a lot better than my short-term one.

"I'm J.T. Murray," said the woman, shaking hands with each of our foursome in turn. "I'm so glad to meet all of you."

"Forgive my being nosy, but what does J.T. stand for?" Claire asked.

J.T. laughed. "My parents wanted a son," she said. "Instead, they got me. So, to compensate, they nick-named me J.T. That's what everyone calls me these days."

I had the distinct impression that Sister Rose was becoming more and more annoyed at the delay in our tour of the facility because of what she viewed as idle chitchat. My impression was solidified by the loud *tap tap tap* of her shoe on the marble floor.

J.T., however, seemed oblivious to Sister Rose's impatience. Turning to Mary Alice, she said, "It's so lovely to meet people who graduated from Mount Saint Francis. I want you to know that our company is committed to keeping as much of the building in its original state as possible."

"J.T., if you please," said Sister Rose in an icy tone. "I distinctly remember telling you that I have an important appointment this afternoon that I cannot be late for. We need to start the tour *right now.*"

J.T. turned to Sister and gave her a brilliant smile. "Of course, Sister Rose. You're the boss."

And in that single second, for reasons I'll never be able to explain to anyone, I realized that I was witnessing a power struggle between two very strong personalities – J.T. and Sister Rose. And perhaps, for the first time in her life, Sister Rose was on the losing end.

Chapter 8

Just like marriage and motherhood,
nothing really prepares you for getting old.

"This is going to be a state-of-the-art facility when it's completed," J.T. said as she led us down the marble staircase toward what used to be our old cafeteria. "Whoops," she said, "please be careful where you're walking. There are obstacles left by the workmen all over the place. Sorry about that."

This last was directed at me. In my own, typically clumsy fashion, I had managed to trip over a paint can that had suddenly appeared in my path. Fortunately, the can was closed tight, so I didn't spill anything on the blue tweed carpeting.

That's what happens when you don't look where you're going. I mean, when I don't look where I'm going. But I felt like I'd been transported to a strange new world – like a tourist visiting New York City for the first time. Instead of gawking at all the tall buildings, though, I was gawking at the freshly painted walls. And the magnificent crystal chandelier that hung in the center of what used to be a dingy, dark hallway.

"This whole area looks bigger than I remember," Claire said. "Didn't there used to be a series of small rooms along this corridor? I think one of them had a piano in it."

"You're right, Claire," said Sister Rose, speaking quickly before J.T. could get a word in. "There were several small rooms on one side, and the other side had two bathrooms. The architect suggested it would be a much more effective, and efficient, use of space to redesign the bottom floor into one large dining room."

"There will be two apartments down here as well," said J.T., not wanting Sister Rose to upstage her as tour-guide-in-chief. She pointed down a left-hand corridor that none of us had noticed. "Down that hallway. They'll be two-bedroom units, with two full baths."

"Wow, sounds luxurious," Nancy said. I could just imagine her designing a brochure to market the place to prospective customers. She linked her arm through J.T.'s. "I don't know if Sister Rose has told you this, but in addition to be a proud alumna of Mount Saint Francis, I'm also a local Realtor."

"A very successful one," I added. "She was very helpful to Jim and me when we put our house on the market last year. We couldn't have done it without her. The house sold so quickly. We were just amazed."

Nancy flashed me a warning, which I interpreted to mean, *Don't tell J.T. that you ended up moving back into your house. Or about finding the dead body in your living room the night before the closing.*

I narrowed my eyes at Nancy and shook my head a little.

Sheesh. Give me a little credit.

"Oh, look, that's the corner of the cafeteria where we had lunch every day," squealed Mary Alice. "Remember, Claire? Our mothers used to make our sandwiches and wrap them in Saran Wrap so they'd stay fresh. And there was always a piece of fruit in my bag. Never chips." She sighed at the memory.

"I remember you used to trade what was in your brown paper lunch bag with Ginny Holloway," Claire said. "She always had chips in her bag."

"Yeah, but she also had very bad skin," Nancy put in. "And you convinced her that eating potato chips would make her skin break out more, so she'd trade with you. I wonder what ever happened to her. Maybe she'll be at the reunion."

"Just to be clear," J.T. said, "there will be very few units for sale here." She flashed an apologetic look at Nancy. "Our company puts the emphasis on rentals. We have a three-month minimum, for a very cost-effective fee."

She mentioned a dollar figure that would have given Jim cardiac arrest. And that was more than our monthly mortgage payment in pricey Fairport, including the exorbitant taxes. Thank goodness he wasn't here.

I staggered back, holding my chest. Sister Rose gave me a disapproving look, which I ignored.

"J.T., I can't imagine who you think would sign on for a rental here. There's no way Jim and I – he's my husband, by the way – could ever afford this."

"The rent is quite reasonable, considering it also includes three gourmet meals a day," J.T. said. "Plus maid service. I bet that's something you've dreamed about having. But, sadly," she sighed theatrically, but not convincingly, "you're all too young. Our target market is seventy-five to eighty."

Well, it was comforting to know that we were still too young for something!

Chapter 9

All men are created equal. To the chagrin of all women.

"I thought visiting our old high school was a terrific idea," Mary Alice said over a cup of coffee at The Paperback Café, one of our favorite local hang-outs. It was after 3:00, so the restaurant's usual mob of customers had trickled to just a few. "I'm so glad we went today. Now I'm really excited about planning our fortieth reunion."

"Sssh," Nancy said. "There's no need to broadcast how old we all are to the whole world. And remember, we're calling it the Ruby Reunion."

"When did we decide that?" Claire asked. "And why?"

Nancy added a touch of blush to her already flawless makeup, then snapped her compact shut. "Because the ruby is the jewel for a fortieth anniversary," she said. "Everybody knows that. And we thought it would be perfect to use the ruby as the symbol for our class reunion."

Claire rolled her eyes. "Funny, I don't remember that conversation at all."

"Well, we agreed," said Nancy, not willing to concede her point. "Now, how about it, Carol? You've been very quiet since our trip to school."

"You're going to help organize the reunion, aren't you?" Mary Alice asked. "It wouldn't be nearly as much fun without you."

I signaled the server for just a splash more of coffee, stalling for time. So far, I hadn't said a word. I bet all of you find this hard to believe, knowing me as well as you do. But, to tell the truth, the visit to our old high school had affected me more than I was willing to admit. Even to my three closest friends.

Especially seeing what used to be the school chapel. Which, according to the architectural plans J.T. shared with us, was being transformed into a combination conference room and activity space.

Gone were the beautiful marble altar and the (very uncomfortable) wooden pews. To be replaced by a dozen individual square tables which, when fit together, would form a large conference table.

Though how and why this would be utilized in a senior living community was not at all clear to me. Maybe for the longest ongoing bingo game in the world?

The architectural rendering J.T. shared did show that the beautiful stained glass windows were to be preserved, as well as the elevated balcony that ringed the chapel. The nuns used to sit there to keep a watchful eye on the students, to be sure we were behaving ourselves during Mass.

So many meaningful events happened in that chapel, in addition to regular religious services. The one that stands out in my mind was the ring ceremony, where our class received our Mount Saint Francis Academy rings at the beginning of our senior year.

I remember how proud I was of that ring, which had the school logo and motto engraved on it. It meant almost as much to me to receive that class ring as it did when Jim asked me to marry him and slipped a diamond ring on the third finger of my left hand.

Stop it, Carol. Pull yourself together.

Then, to my utter embarrassment, two huge tears escaped from my eyes and landed in my coffee.

Plop. Plop.

Followed immediately by a watery deluge that I couldn't hold back.

"Oh, gosh, I didn't want to do that," I sobbed, grabbing a fistful of napkins and mopping my eyes.

"Carol, sweetie, I had no idea that you'd get so emotional about going back to Mount Saint Francis," Nancy said. "If I'd even suspected how upset the trip would make you, I never would have suggested it. I'm so sorry."

She gave my hand a squeeze of affection, then handed me her compact so I could see how terrible I looked. I took the compact, but didn't open it. I am not a complete masochist, and I already knew my eyes were red and swollen from weeping.

Claire looked shocked at my public display of emotion. I don't want to criticize one of my very best friends, but sometimes I wonder if Claire ever allows her emotions to show. Under any circumstances – public or private. If you get my drift.

Mary Alice rummaged in her handbag and came up with some linty tissues that looked like they'd been hiding in the bottom of the purse since our graduation. "Sorry, Carol. This is the best I can do." She held up a tissue and offered it to me. "I think this is clean," she said. "You can use it to wipe the mascara from around your eyes. You sort of look like a raccoon."

"Rats, I thought you had drugs in there, Mary Alice," I said, trying to laugh and taking the tissue. The laugh became a hiccup, unfortunately. Which led to another hiccup. And another. And before I knew it, I was in full-blown hiccup mode. Which I absolutely hate.

"Well, at least you're not crying anymore," Nancy said, giving me a glass of water. "Here, chug this whole glassful down without taking a breath. That always works for me. And then tell us what the heck is going on with you."

"Excuse me for a second," I said, rising from my seat. "I'm headed for the women's room to wash my face. And calm down in private."

I heard Nancy's voice echoing after me. "Do you want anyone to go with you?"

Honestly, that Nancy. When I said I wanted to calm down in private, that's exactly what I meant. I pretended I didn't hear her – a technique I've learned from Jim, who uses it every time I ask him to take out the garbage.

Splashing some cold water on my face definitely helped. And taking long calming breaths did, too. I dried my face and hands, took a look in the mirror at myself and...yuck, what a shock. I'd managed to wash off any remaining mascara, so I no longer resembled a raccoon. But I had no eye makeup on at all, and I looked like I'd just gotten out of bed in the morning. Which is definitely not a pretty sight.

Oh, well.

"Sorry for the drama," I said as I rejoined my friends, all of whom stopped talking as soon as they saw me approaching our table. Like I wouldn't figure out that they'd been talking about me.

I pasted a weak smile on my face. "I do feel better now. And I figured out what upset me so much."

Mary Alice handed me a menu. "Here, Carol. Let's order. Food always cheers me up."

Me, too. As my ever expanding waistline constantly reminded me.

"Food won't do it for me this time," I said. "It reminds me of seeing our high school cafeteria today."

Tears sprang to my eyes again. I brushed them away angrily and tried to explain why I was so upset.

"Ok, here's the deal," I said. "It was hard for me to walk through the school, but when we got to what used to be the chapel, I was overwhelmed. That beautiful altar. Gone. And all the pews, too. That chapel was such a special place for all of us. It just upset me so much. I couldn't deal with it."

Everyone started talking at once. "I felt the same way," Mary Alice said. "But I thought I was overreacting."

"Me, too," said Nancy. "But I didn't want to say anything."

Even Claire nodded her head. "I know exactly what you mean, Carol." And – was I seeing things? – the always unflappable Claire reached for a wad of napkins to stop her tears, which were flowing down her cheeks.

We all began bawling like babies.

"There's nothing like a good cry," Nancy said as our crying jag began to diminish. "I feel a lot better, letting all that emotion out."

"I wonder how Sister Rose feels about the chapel," Mary Alice said. "It must upset her even more than us."

"It takes a lot to upset Sister Rose," Claire said. "Plus, she and the other sisters had to agree to the architectural plan before the renovations began. They've had time to adjust to the changes. For us, it was overwhelming."

The next half hour was spent speculating about how the place was going to look when it was finished, and if the school was the best place to hold our reunion. I guess that meant I was officially on the planning committee.

Nancy suggested a destination reunion. Like a destination wedding, except for geriatrics. But we vetoed that idea when Mary Alice pointed out that "destination" usually meant travel. Which always meant spending money. Which some of our classmates might not have an abundance of these days.

Yak yak yak. The conversation went back and forth. Forever. With nothing being decided. Except the "ruby" theme, of course. Nancy was insistent about that.

But I didn't mind a bit. Because I was off the hook. I didn't have to explain the other reason why I got so upset when we were touring our old high school. And why I'd resisted going to a reunion for years.

And I'm not telling any of you why, either.

Chapter 10

I used to have a handle on life, but it broke.

Ok, I'll tell you. But you have to promise that you won't tell anyone else. I can trust you, right?

Besides, if I find out that other people know my secret, I'll know you squealed on me.

Ok. Again. Here goes.

I've never admitted this to anyone – not Nancy, Claire, Mary Alice, Jim, or my two kids – but when I was a freshman in high school, I was painfully shy. I mean, PAINFULLY shy. It embarrasses me now just to think about it.

When the four of us were in grammar school, it was a pretty small class. We were a tight group of best friends from sixth grade on. And there was no competition among us.

But when we got to Mount Saint Francis, that all changed. And not for the better, from my point of view. Nancy, being the pretty one – well, she was gorgeous, to tell you the truth, and her figure blossomed long before the rest of ours did, so she was beating the guys off with a stick (figure of speech) – immediately became a member of the popular clique. These were the girls with long shiny hair, a luminous complexion (no zits allowed!), straight white teeth (no braces, allowed, either), and above all, no eyeglasses. I'm betting several of this crowd wore them at home, though. But they were just too vain to be seen in public with glasses on. Or, I guess they could have worn contacts.

Anyway.

Claire was the brainiac of our group. She always got straight A's, no matter what the subject was. But she never flaunted her intelligence. And she was always willing to help any of us who might be floundering in a particular subject – like arithmetic, for example. I know this from personal experience.

So, of course, Claire immediately gravitated to the other brainiacs in the class, and they formed a pretty tight group. There were fewer of them than of the popular crowd, however.

Mary Alice was just as sweet when she was a kid as she is now. She's always been a natural caregiver, and everyone loved her. Becoming a nurse was a natural career choice for her. But she was also very organized and a natural leader beneath all that sweetness, so guess what! She was elected president of our freshman class. Which meant she had to attend lots of after-school meetings etc. etc. In fact, Mary Alice was so involved in school functions in freshman year that I wondered when she had time to study.

And that left…me. Literally.

I was left out. Completely. All my grammar school friends moved on when we got to high school, and left me standing alone. All alone. (Cue violins here.)

I know, I know. I'm not the first person this has happened to. And I know I'm not the last one, either.

But this is my story, and no one else's.

So, I was pretty miserable during the first semester of freshman year at Mount Saint Francis. Being shy (and probably self-centered, too), it never occurred to me that there were other girls in my class who were going through the exact same thing. Other girls who could have become my friends. If I hadn't been so stupid.

Classes weren't so bad. But lunch periods were pure torture for me, because I often had no one to sit with. If I got extra lucky, I'd get to the cafeteria and there'd be a seat at Mary Alice's table. To be fair, I know she always tried to save me one.

But sometimes she couldn't.

Both Nancy and Claire were on a different lunch schedule, so sitting with either of them wasn't an option. (Cue more violins.)

I was pretty miserable. So miserable that sometimes I'd skip lunch entirely, sneak out of school, and go for a walk outside. I was an expert at getting out of and back into school without being caught, too. Most of the time.

But when I did get caught, I'd cover up my fear – what was my punishment going to be this time? – by being a smart aleck. Which, of course, got me into even more trouble with the good sisters.

It was all an act, of course. I was doing a shtick, before I even knew what the word meant. And meanwhile, I was absolutely miserable. With no one to confide in.

I wanted so much to tell my mother what was going on. But every time she'd ask me about school, I'd lie and tell her everything was fine. By the way, although I was absolutely miserable, I continued to get good grades. Not as good as Claire's, of course. But certainly respectable enough to make honor roll.

As you can imagine, I had lots of time to study.

And then a new girl transferred into our freshman class. Her family had recently moved from Manhattan to our bucolic suburb of Fairport, Connecticut. Her name was Mary Margaret Mahoney, and if my life was miserable before, after she arrived, things got even worse.

I wonder if any of you have ever looked at a person and instantly despised them. No particular reason – just a mutual, visceral, primal loathing. That's what happened with Meg and me. Oh, yes. Although her name was Mary Margaret, everyone called her Meg.

There was a practical reason for the nickname. In our class, there were nine other girls whose first name was Mary. Mary Louise, Mary Pat, Mary Beth – I'm sure you get the idea. So nicknames became the only way our teachers could keep everybody straight.

As a matter of fact, Mary was the most popular girl's name until the 1960s. I'll bet none of you knew that. Then it fell out of favor, and now, it seems nobody names their daughter Mary anymore. Although variations of the name still pop up, like Maria, Marissa, and Mariah. A bit of trivia you can all use when there's a conversational lull at the next cocktail party you go to.

Anyway, Meg Mahoney made it very clear that she was not to be called Maggie, or, heaven forbid, Peggy. It was Meg. Period.

In no time at all, Meg had completely taken over the popular clique in the freshman class. Everyone wanted to be her friend. Heck, people actually competed to do her homework for her, if you can believe it.

Even the nuns loved her.

In fact, everyone seemed to love her except...you guessed it. Me. And the feeling was mutual. So Meg went out of her way to make my life miserable every chance she got.

I tried not to feel hurt every time Meg would invite a group of girls to do something after school or on weekends– in front of me – and not include me in the invitation. To be fair, though, Mary Alice, Claire and Nancy did turn down those invitations out of loyalty to me.

At least, they told me they did.

Things came to a head the night of our freshman dance. Yes, back in the dark ages, even though Mount Saint Francis was an all-girls' school, we did have dances. Closely supervised by the nuns. And chaperoned by loads of parents.

I didn't have a date, of course. That was long before I met Jim. But Mary Alice didn't have a date, either, and she talked me into going with her. I didn't want to go, but then Nancy and Claire ganged up on me. Both of them had dates, and promised to share them with Mary Alice and me so we could get a chance to dance, too.

I was so excited that night. My mom had taken a hand-me-down dress from an older cousin and refashioned it for the dance. I remember it was powder blue taffeta, which she said brought out the blue in my eyes. Short sleeves, modest neckline. Of course.

I thought it was the most beautiful dress I'd ever had, and I felt like a princess in it.

My special night got even better when I got to the dance. Nancy and Claire had convinced their dates – I don't even remember their names – to buy a corsage for Mary Alice and me, as well as for them. For all I know, the girls (or their parents) paid for the flowers themselves. But the point is, they didn't want us to feel left out.

I was having a wonderful time. I think I danced twice – once with each date. Which was twice more than I ever expected.

And then I heard Meg's voice across the dance floor. "Do you believe what Carol Kerr is wearing? That dress is an absolute disaster. It looks homemade. Or like something from a rag heap." And her faithful acolytes tittered and agreed.

I was humiliated. Beyond anything anyone can possibly imagine. I wanted to fade into the woodwork. Or die, right there. Or even, better yet, have Meg keel over dead from an overdose of punch.

I don't think I've ever hated anyone that much in my whole life, before or since.

And that's my secret. Because being back at Mount Saint Francis today brought that whole ugly night back. And that terrible Meg Mahoney.

So you can imagine I was less than thrilled when Nancy announced that Meg had come back to Fairport after all these years and wanted to help organize our fortieth class reunion.

Chapter 11

Revenge is best served cold with lots of white wine.

I choked on my coffee. Mary Alice immediately jumped up and started pounding me on the back. "Do you have something caught in your throat?" she asked.

I shook my head and continued to cough. And finally managed a raspy, "Just give me a minute and I'll be fine."

"You're not going to cry again, are you, Carol?" Claire asked, concern written on her face despite voicing what could be interpreted by someone who is easily offended (like me) as a criticism. "What's wrong?"

Nancy, bless her, sensing that the curtain was about to rise on Act 2 of my spontaneous dramatic presentation, signaled the server for our check. Which she paid in full, leaving a generous tip.

When Claire and Mary Alice started to chip in some money, Nancy said, "This one's on me." She pushed back her chair and grabbed my coat. "Everybody up. We'll go to my house to see if we can sort this whole reunion thing out in private.

"Come on, Carol. You're coming with me."

And she led us all out of the coffee shop without any arguments from anyone. Even me.

On the ride to Nancy's house, I started to apologize for my outburst, but she silenced me with a wave of her hand. "No need to say you're sorry, Carol. I'm sure you had a good reason for reacting the way you did."

We cruised to a stop at the intersection of Fairport Turnpike and Benton Road, Nancy's street. She gave me a quick look. "I'm betting that you're not just upset about how the school is being renovated. It's more than the chapel being turned into a nightclub for geriatrics, isn't it?"

I managed a tiny smile. "The chapel isn't being turned into a nightclub and you know it."

"Well, a bingo parlor then," Nancy said. The light turned green and in less than two minutes we were parked in Nancy's driveway.

"I think you're hiding something, Carol," my very best friend said to me. "I've always thought there was something that bugged you about Mount Saint Francis. Or, should I say, someone? It's time to let it out.

"I used to think Sister Rose was the problem. But now we've reconnected with her after all these years. And even you have to admit that she's not the ogre we thought she was when we were in high school. In fact, she's very nice. And the program she's running now for domestic violence victims is a fantastic service to the Fairport community."

I exited Nancy's sports car – still another new one, no doubt a business deduction on her next tax return – and headed toward the front door. I was trying to collect my thoughts, because I knew Nancy wouldn't give up on me until I came clean. And Mary Alice and Claire would join right on in, too.

With love, of course.

I knew Nancy was right. It was way past time to clear the air, once and for all. And maybe then, I'd finally feel better. And stop this stupid crying once and for all.

Chapter 12

No use crying over the past.
The older you get, the less you remember.

"We never really had lunch," Nancy said as she came into her sunny conservatory carrying a tray of sandwiches and tea. "Here's some sustenance so we won't starve to death."

Yes, you read that right. Nancy has a conservatory. Remember, she's a Realtor. And when the buy of the century in Fairport real estate (only partially exaggerating) came on the market five years ago – that would be the former home of the late, famous screen star Patricia Helmond – Nancy and her husband Bob snatched it up. Not only did it have views of Long Island Sound, but it did, indeed, have a conservatory.

Jim and I have a deck and a screened-in porch. Just sayin'.

"When did you have the time to make these?" I asked, grabbing a tuna triangle on whole wheat bread and snarfing it down. So sue me. Stress makes me hungry.

Heck, everything makes me hungry.

Nancy looked just a teeny bit embarrassed. "They're actually left over from the garden club meeting here yesterday afternoon. I hope they're not stale. Or soggy."

"They're delicious, Nancy," said Mary Alice, her mouth full of turkey wrap. "Oh, excuse me. I didn't mean to talk with my mouth full."

"Leftovers work fine for me," said Claire, grabbing half an egg salad sandwich with one hand and a napkin with the other.

For the next few minutes, nobody spoke. We were all too busy enjoying an unexpected, and yummy, lunch.

"My thanks to the Fairport Garden Club," said Claire, "for not pigging out yesterday and allowing us to feast on their leftovers. I knew there was something about that bunch I liked, even though I couldn't grow a plant to save my life.

"Now, Carol," she continued, fixing me with a radar stare, "we've all finished eating. You've had time to collect your thoughts. I hope. So what the heck is up with you? And no dodging the question. It's tell-the-whole-truth time."

"You make me feel like I'm in the confessional," I said with a desperate attempt at levity. Which I knew wasn't the least bit funny, but I was stalling for time. I've never been good at getting to the point. Or telling the truth, the whole truth, and nothing but the truth. So help me, God.

I dabbed my mouth with a napkin – another poor excuse to buy time, in case you haven't picked up on that.

"I'm embarrassed," I said.

"Well, you should be," said Claire. "You acted like a real jerk at The Paperback Café."

"I wasn't acting," I shot back. "It's just that...." Tears coursed down my cheeks.

"God, there she goes again," Claire said in disgust.

"Give her a break," said Mary Alice. Then, to me, "Sweetie, you know we all love you. Even Claire, though at this exact moment, she's not acting that way. You can trust us. Whatever is causing your misery, tell us what it is. And I promise you, if we can help you get over it, or fix it, we will."

She turned toward the other two women. "Right?"

Nancy and Claire bobbed their heads in agreement. And Claire took my hand. "I'm sorry if I was rough on you. But it makes me crazy to see you so upset. I want to help you. Really, I do. We all do."

I took a deep breath, and began my story. "Remember freshman year at Mount Saint Francis? How nervous we all were at starting high school? But excited, too."

"Of course we remember," said Nancy. "Right before classes officially started, we had a sleepover at my house. But I don't think any of us got any sleep. We stayed up all night giggling. And talking. And playing records. My mother kept coming in and asking us to turn out the light and go to sleep. Probably so she and Dad could get some sleep, too."

We all laughed at the memory. "I never appreciated how much sleep an adult needs until my sons were born," Mary Alice said. "That's when I understood what being sleep-deprived could do to a person."

We were getting off track here. Not that I'm immune from going off on side tangents myself, understand. But once I'd started this story, I was determined to finish it.

I cleared my throat, then said, "Anyway, that night the four of us made a solemn pledge to be best friends forever. We stood in a circle and held hands. That meant the world to me. I had siblings, at last."

Nancy squeezed my hand. "I know, sweetie. It was tough on you, being an only child and born to older parents. But we're still best friends, after all these years. And I treasure all of you now even more than I did when we were all fourteen."

My eyes misted up again, but this time I controlled myself.

"But we weren't always best friends, Nancy. Freshman year in high school, especially first semester, everyone went their separate ways. At least, that's how it seemed to me."

"What do you mean, Carol?" Claire said. "We were still close."

"Maybe you thought we were close. But I felt that all of you abandoned me for new friends."

There, I'd said it.

"Carol, you are being absolutely ridiculous." From Claire.

"Carol, I never realized you felt that way. I am so sorry if I did anything to hurt you." From Mary Alice.

"Sweetie, you know I love you. But I think you must be exaggerating. Or remembering wrong." From Nancy.

I knew I had to keep going.

"I don't mean to imply that any of you did this deliberately. But, Claire, when we got to high school, you immediately became part of the brainy crowd. As you should have been. I'm not trying to criticize you for being smart. I was so proud to be your friend.

"Mary Alice, when you ran for freshman class president and won, I was thrilled for you. We all were. But then, you had so many after-school meetings and activities that there didn't seem to be a lot of time left over for old friends. And then you joined glee club, and got even busier."

I didn't dare look at Mary Alice. I knew I was upsetting her.

But I was wrong. Mary Alice was angry. At me.

"In case you've forgotten, Carol, my parents made me quit glee club at the end of first semester because my grades started to slip," Mary Alice said. "Freshman year wasn't as great for me as you think it was."

I felt bad for her, but I needed to get all my gripes on the table once and for all. So I soldiered on.

"Nancy, you became so popular, right away," I said. "Everybody wanted to be your friend. You got invited to all the cool parties."

"But Carol," Nancy protested, "I insisted that you be invited, too. That all of you be included, in fact."

"I didn't belong in that crowd, Nancy. And I didn't belong with the smart kids, either. Or the class leaders. I didn't know where I belonged. And I was too shy to try to find new friends. We didn't even get to have lunch together that first semester. Sometimes, I used to skip lunch and sneak outside until lunch period was over, because I had no one to sit with."

"I tried to save you a seat at my table," Mary Alice objected.

"I know you did." I flashed her a grateful smile. "But there were days when that didn't work out. And....let's just say that I got to know the grounds of Mount Saint Francis Academy very well."

"That may be true, Carol. I'm not saying it isn't. But if memory serves me correctly, you also started to write for the school newspaper in freshman year. So you had some other activities, and ways to make friends, just like we did," Claire said.

"And you began to develop that particular brand of sarcasm and rapier sharp wit we've all come to expect from you," Nancy said. "And I say that with admiration, not as a criticism."

"I did start to write for the paper," I said. "But not until second semester of freshman year. It was the only after-school school activity that interested me.

"And as for my so-called sarcasm and rapier sharp wit, I honed those skills as a defense mechanism. So nobody would figure out how shy and miserable I was."

I sighed. "I guess it worked. It fooled all of you."

I took a deep breath. "I suppose you all think I'm nothing but a big crybaby," I said, "carrying on like this after so many years. And, yes, things did get better. I do have some good high school memories. And one more, very bad one to get off my chest. It's about Mary Margaret Mahoney."

"Meg? I never liked her when we were in school," Nancy said.

"What? You must have selective memory, Nancy," I said. "From where I was watching, you did everything you could to be included in the clique of extra popular girls she started when she transferred into our class. Including lending her your very best pearl necklace. I think she had it for a month before you finally got it back. I hope it was worth it for you, to suck up to her that way."

Nancy's face got so red I thought she was going to explode.

"Carol, you are so stupid," she said. "I didn't loan Meg my pearl necklace because I wanted to go to her parties. I did it because she forced me to. I made the mistake of telling her that I'd once snuck out of my house after dark to meet a boy that my parents didn't approve of. She threatened to tell them if I didn't let her borrow my special necklace for as long as she wanted. You don't know beans about my relationship with Meg."

"I didn't like her much, either," said Mary Alice. This coming from a woman who rarely has an unkind word to say about anybody. "At first, when I won the election, she was so supportive. She had lots of suggestions on how our class could be run, and how the school could be improved. Then she figured out that I had very little, if any, clout with the administration. So she dropped me like the proverbial hot potato. And that was the end of our so-called friendship."

"Ha!" said Claire. "I bet I can top that. Meg made it clear that she thought anyone who studied for exams and got good grades was an idiot. Especially me, because I always got the best grade on any test in any subject. She was pretty smart herself, though, and got good grades, too. But never as good as mine. Senior year, she started a rumor among all her so-called 'friends' that the only reason I got good grades was because I cheated on all my tests. And she actually had the gall to go to the principal's office and tell Mother Mary Dolores that I was cheating. And Mother Dolores believed her! Without a shred of evidence! That's why Meg ended up being the valedictorian of our class, and I was the salutatorian. Oooh, just thinking about that makes me so mad!"

Whoa.

"I had no idea that Meg picked on any of you, too," I said. "Why didn't you say something?"

"Ha, coming from you, that's pretty rich, Carol," said Claire, still smarting from the memory of the injustice she suffered 40 years ago. "You didn't say anything to us about your problems, either."

"I don't know about either Claire or Mary Alice, but I was embarrassed to admit that Meg pushed me around that way."

"Compared to what the rest of you suffered from Meg, I got off pretty easy," Mary Alice said. "All she did was drop me as a friend. I think I was lucky, all things considered."

"Carol, you started all this. But you still haven't told us what Meg did to you that was so terrible," Nancy said. "So far, it looks like Claire suffered the most from her. I mean, being accused of cheating. That's terrible! By the way, Claire, what finally happened? Did Meg ever admit she lied?"

"No way," Claire said. "Sister Rose went to bat for me. She convinced Mother Dolores that Meg must have misunderstood something she saw. And she must have 'convinced' Meg of the same thing. Fortunately, the story never got out. I could have been expelled, I guess."

Claire pursed her mouth together to stop her lips from trembling. I could tell that she was close to tears.

"So, Carol, what happened to you? Did Meg tell lies about you, too?" Nancy asked.

"No," I said. "But she publicly humiliated me at the freshman dance."

"What happened at that dance?" Claire asked. "I don't remember anything about it except my date stepping all over my feet and trying to dip me back until I almost fell down on the floor."

"My mother had gone to a lot of trouble to remake a dress that belonged to one of my cousins," I said. "I thought it was the most beautiful dress I'd ever seen. And Meg made fun of me and the dress. Publicly. Loudly. She said my dress looked like something out of a rag heap. Everybody started to laugh at me. And I ran out the door and went home. I've never been so humiliated in my life."

"Where the heck was I?" asked Nancy. "I don't remember any of this."

"This must have happened when the zipper broke on my dress, Claire," Mary Alice said. "You and I went to the bathroom and you pinned me back together the best you could."

"Of course. I remember that now," said Claire. "Although the rip wasn't really that serious."

"You wouldn't have said that if you'd been wearing the dress," said Mary Alice.

"I finally remember where I was, and what I was doing. And with whom," Nancy said, blushing. "No need to bring that up now."

"Carol, that must have been a terrible experience for you. Traumatic," said Mary Alice. "But I'm so glad you finally told us what happened. In fact, I'm glad all of us shared our Meg stories. I don't know about the rest of you, but I'm feeling better already."

"I am, too," I said, surprised that I was telling the truth. "I really am. After all these years of holding that story in."

I turned to Nancy and said, "I can't believe that you want Meg to help us organize the reunion after all she did in high school to make our lives miserable. Sheesh."

"Meg contacted me and offered to help," Nancy retorted, slightly defensive. "I haven't gotten back to her yet. So, what do you all think?"

"I think it's a terrible idea," said Claire.

A phrase popped in my head. I think it was from one of Shakespeare's plays, but it could also be from a movie (*The Godfather* maybe?). Something about keeping your friends close, but your enemies closer. It sounded appropriate for this situation. Maybe it would be better to have Meg on our committee so we could keep an eye on her than have her scheming to wreck the reunion somehow. Paranoia is my middle name.

And that's how I convinced Nancy, Claire and Mary Alice to include Meg on the committee. The committee I promised my three friends I'd be on, too.

What the heck.

Chapter 13

I'm always willing to compromise.
Just as long as we do things my way.

"I suppose you think I'm crazy," I said to Jim over coffee the following morning.

"If you think I'm going to respond to that, you're wrong," Jim said. "After more than thirty years of marriage, I know when to keep my mouth shut."

I leaned over the breakfast table and gave him a quick peck on his unshaven cheek. "You are such a smarty pants. I'm talking about my agreeing to help organize the fortieth class reunion from Mount Saint Francis Academy."

"Am I supposed to be surprised about that?" Jim asked. "Well, I'm not. First of all, Nancy would keep after you until she wore you down. You'd say yes just to get her off your back. And you always love organizing things. Running the show. Telling people what to do. It's one of your most endearing traits."

I resisted the urge to throw a piece of low-salt, fat-free buttered toast at My Beloved. (We're both watching our cholesterol and blood pressure these days.)

"What made you change your mind?" Jim asked. "You were pretty adamant at dinner the other night that you wanted no part of the reunion. You weren't even sure you'd go."

I considered my answer carefully. To share my humiliation at the freshman high school dance with my husband would be a complete waste of time. He'd never get it. Nor would he understand how cathartic it was to finally talk about that incident. And find out that my three closest friends had suffered similar abuse from Meg Mahoney.

In fact, he'd wonder why all the hurts that we'd suffered in high school because of Meg were still bothering us after all these years. And I couldn't blame him, because I didn't know why, either. They just…were.

"Nancy, Claire, Mary Alice and I went back to Mount Saint Francis yesterday," I said. "Sister Rose was there, too. Did I tell you that our school is being turned into a senior living community?

Jim nodded. "I hope you didn't sign us up for a room, Carol."

"Actually, Jim, you'll be pleased to know that the marketing director of the new facility – her name is J.T. something – told us we were all too young to live there now. The target population they're aiming at is aged seventy-five and older."

Jim harrumphed. "It's good to know we're still too young for something."

I ignored his comment. Since I, of course, had thought the exact same thing.

"Anyway, being back at school brought back a lot of memories for me."

Mostly traumatic.

"And after the tour, we went back to Nancy's and talked about old times. Gosh, I can't believe we were ever that young and innocent."

I took a sip of coffee and savored it, while I figured out what to say next.

"Anyway, I decided I wanted to be part of planning the reunion after all. I thought Nancy would faint when I told everybody. And there's at least one other person from our class, Mary Margaret Mahoney, who wants to help."

I almost choked when I said Meg's name, but I didn't. I hope you're all proud of me.

"Mary Margaret Mahoney?" Jim said. "You mean, Meg Mahoney?"

Say what?

"Yes, Jim," I said. "Meg Mahoney. Why? Did you know her?"

Jim wiggled his eyebrows in a suggestive manner. "I'll say I did. We dated for a few months in high school." He sighed. "Boy, she was a real hottie."

Oh, boy. This was all I needed to start my day off wrong. And just when I was starting to feel more secure.

Betrayed by my own husband! The cad.

"I didn't realize you ever dated Meg," I said in as measured a tone as I could manage under the circumstances. I put my coffee cup down before the liquid began to slosh over the rim – my hands were shaking – and gave my husband a cold stare. "She was the bane of my existence in high school. And, as it turns out, was terrible to Claire, Mary Alice and Nancy, too. Why didn't you tell me this before? Or were you trying to hide it from me?"

"Geez, Carol, lighten up," said my clueless husband. "This was more than forty years ago, long before I met you. And we only had a few dates. You never told me about your old boyfriends, either."

If I'm being honest, there wasn't that much to tell. But I wasn't going to admit that to Jim. So I contented myself with glaring at him across the breakfast table.

"What difference could my dating Meg Mahoney all those years ago possibly make now?" Jim said, trying to get himself off the hook he found himself on as quickly as possible. "Why do you care so much?"

Hmm. Good question. Why did I care so much? Maybe because good old Mary Margaret Mahoney was about to re-enter my life, thanks to the fortieth high school reunion committee.

Now I needed to make sure that, just for spite, she didn't nudge her way back into my husband's life, too.

Chapter 14

I'm too young for the senior center. But if you find a junior center, let me know.

"I don't see what all of you are so upset about," Nancy said, pretending to examine the luncheon menu at Maria's Trattoria with deep concentration. "We decided that Meg could help organize the reunion. All I did was follow up and invite her to join us for lunch today."

"I was under the impression we were a committee of equals," said Claire. "It's more like a dictatorship. With you as the dictator, Nancy."

"Well, somebody has to be in charge," Nancy retorted. "If Meg's going to be involved, then I say, the sooner, the better. We can use all the help we can get. If we want to have the reunion in October, right before the senior living community is supposed to open, we don't have a lot of time and we have lots to do. That's what Sister Rose wants, remember?"

"I just think that you should have asked us first, before you invited Meg to lunch," Claire said, not wanting to let her point drop without a fight. Fortunately, the lunch crowd was in full swing at the restaurant and nobody could overhear our conversation.

I snuck a look at Mary Alice. She appeared transfixed by the lunch specials written on the chalk board above Nancy's head. But she wasn't fooling me. She didn't want to get in the middle of this squabble.

Neither did I. But somebody had to step in before Meg arrived and we were all embarrassed.

I put my hand on Claire's arm, squeezed it hard, and said "Stop. Now. As far as I'm concerned, you're both right, and you're both wrong."

I held up my hand for silence. It was my turn to talk.

"Nancy, you were wrong to invite Meg to our lunch without letting us know first," I said. "And, Claire, you're wrong to call Nancy a dictator. She's right. Somebody has to spearhead this reunion. I know we all have old beefs against Meg..."

"I think Meg's lying about me cheating trumps her embarrassing you at a school dance, Carol," said Claire with a sniff.

"You're right, of course," I said in my most soothing tone. The one I used many times when I was attempting to settle a quarrel between Jenny and Mike about whose turn it was to choose which television show to watch.

"But, for your information, Jim told me this morning that he and Meg dated while they were in high school. So not only do I have to deal with someone who tormented me in school, now I find out she's one of my husband's former girlfriends."

I stopped talking for a minute to let the enormity of what I had just said sink in. Then I added, "I have no intention of giving Meg the opportunity to rekindle an old flame. I'm not that crazy. But maybe she's changed. I'm willing to give her a chance. I'm determined to be pleasant to her at lunch today. And if I can do it," I leveled my baby blues directly at Claire, "then you can, too."

Boy, was I proud of myself for convincing everyone I was telling the truth. That I was even willing to let bygones be bygones, as the old saying goes. And give Meg a chance.

I was lying, of course. I was so nervous about seeing Meg again that I didn't know how I would handle it. For all my bravado, I was on Claire's side. And if I had known in advance that Meg was coming today, I probably would have made up an excuse not to come.

I was conscious of a sharp intake of breath to my immediate left. Then a (gentle) kick to my shin. "Don't look now," Nancy said in a low voice. "But I think Meg just walked into Maria's."

Claire immediately swiveled her head around for a good look.

"Don't stare," Nancy whispered.

"For heaven's sake, Nancy. If we don't look, how the heck will we know whether it's Meg or not?" Mary Alice said.

"If it is Meg, she brought another woman with her that I don't recognize. What should we do? Wait for her to recognize us? Stand up and wave like idiots?" I asked.

"Don't be ridiculous, Carol," said Nancy. "I planned ahead and, in case we didn't recognize each other, I brought our old yearbook." She rummaged in her designer tote bag. "There it is. I'm going to hold it up casually and see if she reacts."

"It must be Meg," Claire said. "She's heading this way with a big smile on her face that's as phony as a three-dollar bill. And dragging that other woman along with her."

I shot Claire a warning look to watch what she said. The next thing I knew, I was pulled from my chair and enveloped in a giant bear hug and a cloud of Chanel Number 5.

"Carol Kerr, is that really you?" the woman gushed. "You look absolutely fabulous."

No argument from me. I try to take care of myself. Not as much as Nancy does, of course. *Nobody* takes care of herself like Nancy does.

I extricated myself from Meg's grasp. "Nice to see you again, too, Meg. But it's Carol Andrews now. I married Jim Andrews. I think you knew him when we were in high school."

"Jimmy?" Meg exclaimed. "You married Jimmy? Oh, what doll he was. We had so much fun together. I've often wondered what happened to him."

Well, now you know.

"And we have two wonderful children," I added. "Our daughter Jenny was recently married on Nantucket to a Fairport police detective, Mark Anderson. Our son Mike owns a fabulous restaurant in Miami, Cosmo's. Jim and I live in a beautiful antique house right here in Fairport."

Sheesh, Carol. What'd you tell her that for? What if she invites herself over to say hello to "Jimmy"?

I needn't have worried. Meg was far too busy working her way around the table, hugging each woman in turn, to hear the last part of what I'd said.

I turned to the person who was with Meg and said, "Hi. I don't think we've been introduced. I'm Carol Kerr. Well, Carol Andrews now. We went to high school with Meg."

The woman laughed. "You went to high school with me, too, Carol. Don't you recognize me?"

Nope. Not a clue.

I didn't really say that, of course.

"I'm Neecy, Carol. Neecy Nolan. Well, Neecy Prentiss now."

"Neecy?" I repeated? "You're Neecy? Why, I never would have known you. You've changed so much. You look fabulous!"

"I try to go by my real name now, Carol. It's Denise. But nobody ever called me that in high school. Even the nuns."

I used to call you Nosy, because you were always overhearing things that were none of your business and then reporting back to Meg.

I didn't really say that either, of course.

But with Nosy Nolan here at lunch, I was going to watch what I said.

Very very carefully.

Chapter 15

Dear Lord, help me to say the things I should say, not the things I shouldn't. And give me the wisdom to know the difference.

"Isn't this nice?" Meg said, beaming at the rest of us like the queen addressing her court. "Being here together, after all these years.

"Although I have to wonder," she continued, wrinkling up a perfect nose that definitely had been worked on, "why we're meeting here, of all places. There are so many more fashionable restaurants in Fairport. With better food, too. Every time I walk by here, the overpowering smell of garlic makes me gag."

I wondered if Meg said that for spite, because Nancy had chosen the restaurant. But, to be fair, it was possible that Meg had a delicate stomach and the odor of garlic really bothered her. It does happen.

Or, did Meg still have moments where she was totally, completely rude?

I decided not to jump to any quick conclusions. I hope I get points for that.

At the exact moment that Meg had voiced her negative comment, Trattoria owner Maria Lesco was walking toward our table. And Maria was close enough to overhear what Meg had said about her beloved restaurant.

She gave Meg a look that...well, let's just say it's surprising Meg didn't keel right over onto the white linen tablecloth. Nobody says negative things about a restaurant opened by a retired Fairport school teacher, especially one who knows everything about just about everyone in town.

Gracious woman that she is, Maria chose to ignore Meg's remark and greeted the rest of us like the old friends, and good customers, we were. "Wonderful to see you here. I hope you enjoy your lunch. Please let me know if you need anything." Then she swept away in the direction of the open kitchen, where she could keep a watchful eye on us. And everyone else in the restaurant.

But I had seen the look in Maria's eyes. I was sure she was committing Meg's face – and her very bad manners – to memory. And I wouldn't want to be in Meg's shoes if she decided to come back to the restaurant for a meal.

Nancy jumped in to fill the lag in the conversation. "Why don't we order? We all," gesturing to Mary Alice, Claire, and me, "come here a lot. It's a wonderful place, Meg. They do Caesar salad better than anywhere I've ever been. With grilled shrimp on top. It's positively heavenly."

"Works for me," I said, snapping my menu shut. "Me, too," echoed Mary Alice and Claire.

"Well, then," Meg said with a smile, "I guess it will work well for you and me, too, Neecy. Right?"

Well, of course Neecy said yes. No one ever offered a difference of opinion to Meg's. About anything.

There was an awkward silence. Well, there would be, when you have six former classmates, some of whom hadn't seen each other in forty years, together again. Especially since four of the women hated the guts of one of the others.

Then, everyone started talking at once. "What have you been doing all these years?" "Where have you lived?" "You mean you never left Fairport? Well, it is a lovely place." "Did you marry?" "Have any children?" "Of course, I'd love to see pictures of the family."

And on and on.

Not all of this was from the same person, of course. Just a general q. and a. Mostly friendly. Mostly.

Interspersed with occasional nervous laughter.

I didn't say much. I'll bet that surprises you. But I wanted to sit back and really look at Meg, to find out what it was about her that had intimidated me so all those years ago. And see if she still prompted the same insecurities in me as she did in high school.

I had already seen a prime example of adult Meg in action. Her total lack of manners made me cringe.

But did she still have the power to intimidate me? And did I have to worry about her trying to rekindle that old spark with "Jimmy"?

What I saw was a very well preserved woman in her late fifties. Her face was so tight that I bet she'd had work. Botox, at the very least. Maybe even a total face lift. I made a mental note to ask Nancy her opinion about that in private. She's our resident expert on nipping and tucking. Meg was not overly thin. Not overly fat. Just...normal. Someone who seemed comfortable with herself and her life. Not that she'd revealed too much about what she'd been doing for the past 40 years. She seemed much more interested in what the rest of us had been up to.

Her poker straight white hair was styled short in a blunt cut, the kind that, if you shake your head, just naturally falls back into place. I love Deanna, my own personal hairstylist, but she's never been able to get my hair to do that.

Of course, that could be my hair's fault, not a lack of skill on Deanna's part.

Anyway, I looked at this woman who had made my life so miserable, and I found I couldn't hate her. Oh, I wanted to. At first, I wanted to take her Caesar salad and dump it over her head, to pay her back for causing me such public humiliation.

Then, I realized I was finished with all that. I had wasted far too many years brooding about something that was, really – in the overall scheme of life and death – very trivial. And I had allowed Meg to exercise power over me all that time, without her ever knowing it. Which was not only ridiculous, it was downright embarrassing.

And Jim and I had a solid marriage. Not that we didn't have our ups and downs and spats over the years. But since his retirement, which I had dreaded, we'd settled into a nice, cozy rhythm. With only a few issues that still needed to be ironed out, like his taking over the laundry (he never separates colors), and his ongoing reorganization of the kitchen.

But Jim had surprised me by completely redoing the antique house I loved so much and making it more livable for people our age, which was a huge financial investment on his part. This from a man whose obsession with coupons was a legend in Fairport retail establishments.

I looked around the table at my three best friends. All of them, Claire included – who did, after all, have the biggest gripe against Meg – seemed to be chatting away with her and Neecy with no apparent tension. If they could do it, I could, too, by golly.

So I finally grew up and let the Powder Blue Dress Disaster go, once and for all. And I resolved not to obsess about the possibility of Jim dumping me for Meg. Which would take major retraining of my overactive imagination, but I would do it, by golly!

Better late than never, right?

"So, Carol, what's new with you?" Nosy – I mean, Neecy – Nolan asked me as our lunch began to wind down to the inevitable headache of figuring out the bill. "I must say, the years have been kind to you."

I laughed, slightly self-conscious. "That's very kind of you, Neecy. Can I still call you that? I remember you said you prefer to be called Denise now."

"I don't mind an old friend calling me Neecy," she said. "But if I'm introduced to someone as 'Denise,' and that person thinks she can call me Neecy, that bothers me. I suppose if that's the worst thing in my life right now, I should be grateful."

"I know what you mean," I said. Although I had never in my whole life been called anything but Carol. It's one of those names that's hard to substitute a nickname for.

"Did you stay in Fairport?" I asked. "I guess I have no sense of adventure. Except for a brief stint in New York City after college, I've lived here my whole life. Married a local guy, raised two kids, did freelance writing and editing. It's been a good life. But a dull one, I guess."

You'll probably notice that I left out the part about my amateur detective career. It hasn't been my career path of choice, and with any luck, I won't be stumbling over any more dead bodies for the rest of my life. I hope.

"Not a dull one, Carol," Neecy said. "It sounds lovely."

"What about you, Neecy? Do you still live around here? Have you and Meg kept in touch all these years?"

Neecy looked down at her coffee cup. I got the impression that I'd put her on the spot with what I thought were a few innocent questions.

"I got married very young," Neecy said after a long pause. She looked around the table to see if anyone else was listening to our part of the conversation, but Mary Alice and Nancy had left for the women's room (yes, we often go in pairs), and Meg and Claire were now discussing the tip.

"I married Tony Prentiss," Neecy said. "Do you remember him, Carol? He went to Fairport High, and he had a reputation as a wild boy back in those days. In fact, he used to pick me up after school on his motorcycle."

I shook my head. "No, I can't say I knew him. Did he ever come to any of our school dances?"

"You must be kidding, Carol," Neecy said. "My parents would have had a fit. We only started dating publicly the summer after we graduated from high school. After I turned eighteen."

My eyes widened. It seemed like Neecy was admitting she had snuck around dating a boy her parents didn't approve of. Who'd have thought it? And then she married him.

"We eloped that fall," Neecy said. "My parents didn't speak to me for months. Not until the baby came." She colored slightly. "He was premature."

I'll bet.

I didn't really say that, of course. Give me some credit for knowing when to keep my mouth shut.

"Anyway, Tony worked very hard to support us. He had a good head for business, and one thing led to another."

Neecy smiled. "He started his own construction company, and in the beginning, I used to come into the office with the baby and handle the secretarial part of the business. Those were good days. Happy days. Pretty soon, we didn't have to worry about money anymore, and Tony didn't want me to work in the office. He hired a full-time secretary, and then another, to handle the volume of work that started to come in. So I ended up joining a few local women's clubs and trying to do some good work in the community. Truthfully, I was bored. But I didn't let him know that."

She gave me a quick look. "Speaking of being bored, I hope I'm not boring you with my life story, Carol. I didn't mean to go on like this."

"You're not boring me at all, Neecy," I said with a rare flash of insight. It had suddenly occurred to me that Neecy was telling me how lonely she was. And I'd bet anything that she hadn't had a chance to share anything about her life with anybody, for a long time. Thereby proving that money doesn't buy happiness. Or best girlfriends. I couldn't imagine my life without Nancy, Claire and Mary Alice.

Neecy gave me a quick smile. "Tony started building planned communities back in the nineties, when the new construction boom was at its peak. From there, it was an easy segue into building communities for people over fifty-five, with so many boomers as potential customers.

So he started Dockside Living as a subsidiary of Prentiss Construction. It's been even more successful than he dreamed. And when Sister Rose and the other sisters approached him about converting Mount Saint Francis into a senior living community, he jumped at the chance."

"You mean your husband's company is redoing our old high school? And will manage it for the sisters?"

"That's right, Carol. It really is a hoot, when I think about it. I could end up living in our old biology lab in my twilight years!"

"Perish the thought," I said, grimacing. "I was always terrible in that class."

Nancy, back from the powder room with fresh lipstick and a determined look on her face, tapped on a water glass to get everyone's attention. "All right, everyone. This lunch has been a great starting point for our reunion. But if this event is going to happen before the school officially re-opens as a senior living community, we have a lot of work ahead of us and not much time. We need to set another meeting – a working meeting – within the next week. Who will host?"

And just like that, I heard my own voice say, "I will, Nancy. How's this coming Friday at noon for everyone?"

Sometimes I think I should just carry duct tape in my purse, so I can use it to tape my mouth shut when I say stupid things like that.

Rats.

Chapter 16

What part of "woof" don't you understand?

"Maybe having the committee here for lunch on Friday won't be too bad," I said to Lucy and Ethel later that afternoon. "But I'm going to have to clean like a demon to get the house in shape for company. You'll both have to pitch in, too. No slobbering food or water outside your bowls, or dragging in dead things from the yard. Yuck."

Both dogs gave me a look I've come to know very well. Implying that it was not the canines in the Andrews house who were responsible for any lack of cleanliness or order. That responsibility, or blame, rested firmly on the humans who were allowed to reside here, too.

I got the message, loud and clear. If you don't think dogs can communicate with their humans, you've not been paying attention.

"All right, we'll all pitch in."

I rummaged in the broom closet (yes, we still have one – it's a very old house, remember?) for the vacuum. No time like the present to start the house cleaning. I used to have a cleaning service BJR (Before Jim's Retirement), but now, we're watching our pennies and that luxury has gone by the wayside.

I started to assemble the vacuum, then realized how tired I was. I looked at the clock and realized it was almost 4:00, much too late to start a major project like this.

See how easily I can talk myself out of physical exertion? It's an art that I've perfected after years of practice.

Assembling a quick supper held more appeal. As soon as I fed Lucy and Ethel their kibble, of course. I know who comes first in this house.

As I filled their bowls and put them and the dogs in their respective crates (Lucy is a terrible food thief), I brought the dogs up to date on the day's lunch. I can tell the dogs things that I wouldn't tell anybody else and feel comfortable that they won't blab. Or if they do, it'll only be to other neighborhood dogs, so I don't care.

"I was really dreading it," I admitted. "But it wasn't so bad after all. Facing Meg again after all these years wasn't a bit traumatic. Imagining it and worrying about it for so long was much worse.

"It was probably like you two being so scared by that German Shepherd who lives around the corner. When you see that he's out in his yard, you insist on going the other way. Just once, we ought to walk by that house. I bet you'll see he's not so scary after all."

No response from either canine. They were too busy wolfing down their supper.

Too bad I couldn't just open a bag of dry something-or-other and pour it into bowls for Jim and me. Somebody should come up with instant dinner for humans. Bet she'd make a fortune.

"You'll never guess who's coming to lunch here on Friday, Jim," I said, ladling a second generous portion of my homemade vegetable soup into his bowl. Fortunately, Jim isn't at all fussy about what he eats, just as long as there's plenty of it. So the fact that I'd found the soup hiding way back in the dark recesses of the freezer for heaven knows how long didn't bother him at all. A quick nuke in the microwave and dinner was served.

Of course, the nice cabernet wine that I'd uncorked to go along with the scratch meal helped a lot, too. Not only were we drinking it with dinner, but I'd thrown some in the soup, too.

Jim raised his head, spoon halfway to his mouth. Then said, in an extremely reasonable tone, "Well, if I won't guess who's coming to lunch, does that mean you don't want me even to try?"

Smarty pants.

I took a few spoons full of soup myself, marveling at how good it tasted after all this time. I do have a way with leftovers.

"I bet I can guess," My Beloved said. "Spencer Tracy and Katharine Hepburn."

"Very funny, Jim," I said, immediately catching his reference to a wonderful movie starring two of my very favorite actors of all time. "That was *Guess Who's Coming To Dinner,* not to lunch."

I paused and took a small sip of cabernet.

"I'm hosting the first official meeting of the fortieth high school reunion committee here for lunch on Friday," I said. "Nancy, Claire, and Mary Alice, of course. And someone I don't think you've met, Neecy Nolan. Or, I should say, Neecy Prentiss.

"Oh, and one more person," I said, trying to appear casual and knowing that I wasn't. "Someone you know, dear. And haven't seen in a long time. Meg Mahoney."

Jim raised his eyebrows so high they almost disappeared into his receding hairline. "Meg Mahoney? Nice of you to include her on the committee."

Now, let me just interrupt myself to say that a man's reaction to a bombshell announcement like I just made is completely different than a woman's. Am I right? A woman would have immediately bombarded me with questions as to how Meg looked after all this time, did she marry, have any children, where was she living, etc.

Not a man, though. At least, not my man.

Instead, Jim backed up the conversation to a previous name. Neecy's.

"Did you say that your classmate Neecy's last name is Prentiss? Do you know if she's married to Tony Prentiss, the big-wheel property developer?"

"Yes, Jim, she is. They got married soon after graduation. Neecy said his company has diversified into the senior living market which is huge these days, with so many boomers approaching or are already at retirement age.

"His company, Dockside Living, is redoing Mount Saint Francis, and they'll be managing it for the sisters. Isn't that an incredible coincidence?"

"I think Tony Prentiss was a year or two ahead of me in high school," Jim said. "I hadn't made the connection before. I think his name's been mentioned recently as a possible candidate for state senate."

He pushed his chair back from the table. "I going to check him out online while you get out the dessert."

Dessert? Who mentioned anything about dessert? Certainly not me. But I was lucky enough to come up with a half-gallon of Neapolitan ice cream that was visible in the freezer once I had moved out the old soup. Hopefully, it hadn't succumbed to freezer burn. But no matter what, topping ice cream with a gob of fudge sauce is a great cure-all.

By the time I had added some non-dairy whipped topping and a cherry to our makeshift sundaes, Jim was back. "I was right, Carol. Tony Prentiss is a pretty big deal now. It's likely that he'll make a run for state senate, and nobody thinks he'll have any problems securing the nomination.

"You know," Jim continued, "with Meg coming to lunch on Friday, and Neecy Prentiss too, maybe you should call our old cleaning service tomorrow and see if they can send someone to do the house. That'd be one less thing for you to worry about."

Whattaguy, wanting to take the burden of housecleaning off me, even though money was a little tight these days.

"Great idea, Jim. I'll call the office first thing in the morning and throw myself on their mercy."

It wasn't until I was lying in bed next to Jim that night, listening to his rhythmic snoring, that I wondered why he suggested I hire a professional housecleaner. Could it be because he didn't think I'd do a good enough cleaning job myself to impress his old girlfriend?

I always tend toward the worst possible scenario. That way, when it doesn't happen, I'm pleasantly surprised.

I tossed and turned, thumping my pillow, so Jim would wake up. I wanted to confront him with my suspicion about his ulterior motive in hiring the cleaning service. But, of course, he was dead to the world. Figuratively speaking.

I finally gave in and dropped off to sleep myself. And had dreams of Meg showing up for lunch a day early, when the house was still a mess, wearing white gloves and carrying a feather duster. Accompanied by my darling husband, who took her on a complete tour of all the dust bunnies in the house.

The stinker.

Chapter 17

I won't stand for idle gossip. I prefer to sit down so I can relax and really listen.

"I hope you don't mind that I'm a half hour early for lunch," Neecy said, standing at my front door looking slightly embarrassed. "I had to bring Porter to the vet for a shot and it was too far to go back home and drop her off before I came here."

Well, yes, I did mind. But my parents raised me to be polite, under any circumstances. Not that I haven't been known to bend the boundaries of politeness under certain circumstances. Like when somebody really annoys me.

I craned my neck in the direction of Neecy's brand new Range Rover, which was parked right smack in front of my house. This would definitely raise my image among all the neighbors.

"Is Porter a cat or a dog?" I asked.

"She's a beautiful chocolate lab, and I love her to pieces," Neecy said. "Tony gave her to me to fill a huge void in my life when.... Never mind about that. She'll be fine in the car. I took her for a short walk around the neighborhood before I rang your doorbell. And she has a nice bowl of water and some biscuits to snack on."

"I love dogs," I said. "As a matter of fact, we have two spoiled English cockers who pretty much run things around here, Lucy and Ethel," I said. "Right now they're in the master bedroom, complaining bitterly about the cruelty of being incarcerated. And probably lounging all over our bed.

"But I'm forgetting my manners. Please, come in. I hope you don't mind my putting you to work, since you're the first one here." And without giving Neecy, whom I barely knew, a chance to reply, I handed her nine linen napkins.

"Would you be a sweetie and put these out for me? I'm running behind schedule. Nancy called me at eight o'clock this morning to tell me she'd invited three more of our classmates to be on the committee. And they're coming to lunch today. I had to rethink the menu, and come up with something to feed nine people instead of six.

"You know the old saying, the more the merrier, right? Well, we're going to be very merry. Mary Catherine Cosgrove is coming, along with Mary Beth Walsh, and Mary Ann Gisolfi. Maybe I should say, the more Marys, the merrier?"

I was trying to hide my exasperation at Nancy's cavalier decision to add three more people to our committee without consulting the rest of us. When I reacted negatively – Very Negatively – to Nancy's early morning phone call, she informed me that we needed an odd number of committee members whenever we voted on anything. It took all the self-control I could muster not to snap back and ask her when we were going to get to vote on anything, since she seemed to be making all the decisions herself.

"How the heck did we ever keep all these Marys straight?" I asked.

"Even the nuns got confused sometimes, I think," Neecy said, taking the napkins from me and heading toward the dining room. "I'm glad to help you, Carol. This is fun."

"Fun?" I asked. "Setting a table is fun?"

"I suppose you think I'm a little crazy," Neecy said. "And I don't mean to brag. Really. But since Tony's become so successful, I've had a housekeeper to do these things for me. It may sound silly to you, but I've really missed doing these simple things around the house. Now, what else do you want me to do?"

I'm never one to refuse help when it's offered. Especially when I'm under a time crunch.

"Here," I said, handing Neecy a head of romaine lettuce. "Wash this, break it into small pieces and throw it in this salad bowl."

"Got it," Neecy said. "Will do."

And between the two of us, by the time everyone else arrived, lunch was all set.

"Ask me to help you anytime," Neecy whispered in my ear.

"Be careful," I whispered back as I took Claire's coat and hung it in the closet. "I just might."

"So," Nancy said, "let's get down to business. Are we all in agreement about the reunion date? The first Saturday in October? And we'll do a luncheon at school."

She looked around my dining room table, daring any of us to disagree.

Mary Alice, to my utter amazement, spoke up. "Are we just including students from the class? What if some people want to bring spouses? Or...whatever."

Interesting question, especially coming from Mary Alice, who had been a widow for years. I wondered if that online dating site she'd registered on was producing some results that she hadn't told us about.

Not that I'd ever pry, of course. That's completely against my nature.

Nancy beamed at Mary Alice. "I'm so glad you brought that up. It seems to me that the reunion lunch would be much more fun if only our class members attended. But we could have a cocktail party that evening at a local restaurant, like Maria's Trattoria. That way, we could include significant others. What do you all think of that idea?"

"I have another suggestion," Meg said.

I'll just bet you do. I didn't really say that, but I sure wanted to.

"How about if we do the reunion lunch on Sunday, and have the cocktail reception on Saturday night at a local restaurant? That way, we'd all have the chance to break the ice a little before the official reunion event at school."

It killed me to admit it, but that idea had some merit.

"Perhaps another restaurant choice would be better," Meg went on. "We don't want everyone reeking of garlic. Maria's menu choices are very limited."

"I totally disagree," said another one of the Marys. Perhaps Mary Beth? Although the three new additions to the committee looked nothing like each other, neither did they look like people I remembered from school. And since it never occurred to me to put out nametags, I was having some trouble keeping everyone straight.

"I love Maria's Trattoria," she said. "I think that would be a terrific choice for an informal Saturday night get-together." She looked at Nancy. "It would be informal, right? If husbands came, they wouldn't have to wear a jacket and tie, would they?"

"I couldn't get Jim to wear a jacket and tie these days even if I got down on my knees and begged him," I said. Not that anyone was listening to me. Everyone was fixated on the Nancy vs. Meg duel for control of the reunion committee.

"I agree with you, Mary Beth," said Nancy, not one to let Meg take over the meeting without a fight. "Maria's is one of my favorite restaurants, too."

"I also have another great idea for a reunion event that I know you'll all love," Meg continued as if no one else had spoken. She frowned for a minute, then said, "We'd have to find a very private place, though. But it would be a great ice breaker."

She beamed at us. "Are you ready for my other great idea? A pole dancing class! It's fabulous exercise, and we'd have a load of fun. Don't you all just love it?"

Whoa. Talk about bringing a roomful of post-menopausal women to complete silence. Even me. I mean, I'd heard of pole dancing, of course. I'm not a complete Neanderthal. But it was not a dance style I planned to pursue. Ever.

"I think pole dancing is a terrible idea," Claire finally said. "And completely inappropriate for a Catholic high school reunion."

"I agree with Claire," Mary Alice said. "I do, too," Neecy echoed.

"Well!" Meg huffed. "I guess no one is up for new and interesting experiences for this reunion. It's just going to be the same old boring hello, you-look-great, you-haven't-changed-a-bit event."

"There's nothing wrong with that," Mary Alice insisted. "In fact, there's nothing I'd like more than an opportunity to get together with old friends and catch up. I can't wait. I vote no on pole dancing. If we're taking a vote."

And she looked at Nancy, who took the hint. "All those in favor of a pole dancing class as part of our reunion, please raise your hands."

One hand went up. No surprise that it was Meg's.

"Opposed?"

Nancy glanced around at the seven other people (besides herself, of course) who were raising their hands. "Looks like we won't be having pole dancing on the reunion agenda. But thanks, Meg, for suggesting it."

Meg just sat there, her arms crossed and her face looking thunderous. Breathing heavily. Then she stood and announced, "I'm out of here. Plan your own damn reunion. I may not even come."

And she walked out.

Silence.

Then Claire said, "Same old Meg. It's so comforting to know that some things never change. If she can't have her own way, she heads for the nearest highway."

Someone – possibly Mary Ann – tittered. And Mary Alice said, "You just made up a poem, Claire. You're a poet and you don't know it."

And before I could add one of the witty comments I'm famous for, everybody else dissolved into a fit of laughter.

When we all calmed down – we voted to act like we were grown-ups, although for some of us, it was a stretch – it was time for coffee and the rest of the meeting's (that is, Nancy's) agenda.

Mary Catherine raised her hand. Nancy looked at her and said, "We're not in school anymore, Mary Catherine. You don't have to raise your hand to speak."

That set us of giggling again. Nancy rapped on her water glass. "Come on, folks. Let's get a grip here.

"Mary Catherine, what did you want to say?"

"I was just wondering how we're going to let people in our class know about the reunion," she said. "I don't know about the rest of you," Mary Catherine looked around the table, "but I haven't seen most of the class in forty years. Which brings up an interesting point, come to think of it, Nancy. How did you find us? I know that you and Claire and Carol and Mary Alice have all kept in touch, but what about the rest of us?"

Nancy looked so smug I almost belted her. "I have a secret source," she said. "The Realtors' network. As some of you know, I'm a real estate agent in Fairport. I've been keeping track of any realty transactions that involved a member of our class for the past four years. It's not a perfect system, but it's a place to begin. Plus there are websites like classmates.com that we can use."

"I think that site makes a person register first, and give out personal information, before you can find anything out," Claire said. "And there may be a registration fee, too."

Nancy frowned. "Then let's put that site on hold for now." She looked at her notes and continued, "I'm betting Sister Rose will have some ideas about finding people, though. For all we know, she's been keeping tabs on us all these years."

That provoked another round of giggles. And a quick update from Nancy and me as to what Sister Rose was up to these days.

"At least she's not terrorizing innocent students anymore," Mary Beth said. "She was one tough teacher."

"Now, let's talk about a theme for the reunion," Nancy said, determined to keep us on track. "I suggest we call it the Ruby Reunion, because ruby is the stone for fortieth anniversaries. What do you all think?"

I found myself zoning out of this part of the meeting. I'd heard this idea before, and I knew Nancy would get her way. She usually does.

I looked around my dining room table at my former classmates. I realized, to my complete surprise, how glad I was to be part of planning this reunion. And what a terrific group of women had been in my high school class. What a gift to be able to reconnect with them after all these years.

Except for Meg, of course. I'm not a masochist.

My mind wandered, all on its own, down the Meg track. I wondered what she'd been up to all these years since we graduated from Mount Saint Francis Academy. She'd been full of questions for the rest of us about our lives, but offered precious little about her own life. Which was weird, since she was such a show-off in high school, and couldn't wait to share every detail about her wonderful life with the rest of us peons.

I wondered if Neecy knew, and I decided to figure out a way to ask her. First, of course, I'd thank her for her help today. The third degree would follow after a decent interval.

Then, my thoughts returned to Meg's childish behavior, storming out of the meeting when she didn't get her own way about the pole dancing. I hoped that she wouldn't be crazy enough, or mad enough, to try to ruin our class reunion.

Just for spite.

Chapter 18

I never bear a grudge. At my age, I can't remember who I'm mad at, let alone why.

Everyone except Nancy pitched in to clear the table and clean up after the reunion meeting. She made a quick exit, citing an appointment with a potential buyer for a property she'd listed more than a year ago. And since we all knew how tough the real estate market was these days, even though Fairport is on Connecticut's so-called Gold Coast – meaning where the big bucks are in the Nutmeg State – no one tried to stop her.

Or made a snide remark about her getting out of doing the dishes for what was, essentially, a meeting she had called. (That would be me, in case you didn't get that.)

After everyone else had left, I insisted that Neecy let Porter out for a romp around our fenced-in back yard. And, keeping my fingers crossed, I let Lucy and Ethel out to join her.

I kept my fingers crossed because I'm never sure how my dogs are going to react when another dog – especially another female – is off-leash on their turf.

But to my utter amazement – and relief – the three girls got along famously, running around the yard like old friends.

"I guess Lucy and Ethel like other members of the Sporting group," I said to Neecy, referring to the way the American Kennel Club classifies dogs. "If Porter had been in the Terrier or Hound group, I doubt they would have been so welcoming."

"It's funny how dogs gravitate to others who like them," Neecy said. "Too bad people aren't as intuitive as dogs are. We often make bad choices. At least, I certainly have."

I let that remark sink into my brain for a beat or two, not quite sure how to respond. But I sensed it could be an opening for a conversation about Meg, so I plunged ahead.

"Thanks so much for helping me out today, Neecy," I said, throwing a tennis ball in the general direction of the three dogs. As usual, my pitch fell short, and Lucy gave me a dirty look before she ran to get it. Like me, she eschews most forms of exercise.

"I'm really excited about how the reunion is shaping up. I think everybody is."

Neecy snorted. "Yeah, everybody but Meg. Who, of course, had to create a scene when she didn't get her own way."

Careful, Carol. You could be on uncharted waters here. Just this one time, don't stick your foot in your mouth.

"Well, I didn't want to be overly critical," I said, "but since you brought this up, I thought Meg's behavior was pretty childish. One of the important things parents should teach their kids is that nobody gets their own way all the time. That's just the way life works."

Of course, I agreed. In principle. Not that this stops me from trying to have my own way as much of the time as possible. But in a much more adult, and subtle way. Of course.

"I don't want to keep you, Neecy," I said. "But the three dogs are having such a good time running around the yard and chasing sticks and heaven knows what else, that I hate to break this up."

"Don't worry about my schedule, Carol," Neecy said. "Truthfully, I don't have one today. Tony will be at the office all day. Or maybe at one of his construction sites. And then he'll probably head to a political meeting. I doubt he'll even be home for supper. But if you have things you want to do, please don't let Porter and me intrude. We can go to the beach and she can run around there for a little while."

"I don't think so, Neecy," I said. "It's after April first, and the town of Fairport, in its infinite wisdom, has closed off beach access to dogs until the end of October."

I pulled out a lawn chair which Jim had left propped up against the side of the house.

Please feel free to insert a comment here about my husband never putting things away where they belong once he's finished with them. I don't mind a bit. In fact, maybe if you said something to him, he'd pay attention. Heaven knows, he ignores me.

"Have a seat, Neecy," I said. "I'll sit on the steps."

Neecy took the chair with a little hesitation. "If you're sure you don't mind our staying a little longer, I will." She winced as she sat on the chair's hard seat. "My pills are wearing off. Good thing I always carry some in my purse."

When I returned from the kitchen with a glass of cold water, Neecy didn't look well at all. Her face was pasty white, and she was starting to shake.

Neecy grabbed the glass from my hand and downed two oval white pills in one swallow. Then she took a deep breath, leaned back in the chair and closed her eyes.

I took the glass from her hand and just stood there, watching her like a dope. I felt so helpless. Gradually, the color returned to her face and she opened her eyes.

"Thanks, Carol," Neecy said. "I feel much better now. Sorry to be so much trouble."

"Trouble? Don't say that, Neecy. You're no trouble. I'm just glad I was able to help you. Does this happen often? Oh, my God, what if this had happened to you when you were driving?"

Neecy gave me a weak smile. "Don't worry, Carol. This was an especially bad pain attack. I was having so much fun at the reunion planning lunch that I forgot to keep to my regular med schedule. I doubt it will happen again. Just give me a minute to catch my breath."

I sat down on the step. "Take all the time you need. I'm glad to have the chance to talk to you more, and I had no plans for the rest of the afternoon." I waved in the general direction of the three frolicking canines. "Besides, as you can see, the three dogs are having a terrific time. I haven't seen Lucy and Ethel run around this much in a long time. I bet that when you try to put Porter back in your car, they'll start to cry."

I laughed at Neecy's puzzled expression. "I'm kidding. Really. But maybe, since the dogs are getting along so well, we should arrange to get them together on a regular basis. What do you think?"

"What a great idea, Carol," Neecy said. She started to get up from the chair and winced. "Damn it. I think I'd better sit here a little while longer. I'm still in some pain, but it's subsiding."

"I don't mean to pry," *much,* "but what happened to cause you such pain? Did you have a car accident? Or a bad fall?"

"I had a skiing accident," Neecy said. "About two years ago." She closed her eyes briefly. "It was pretty terrible. In fact, I almost died. But thanks to some great doctors, and a long period of rehabilitation, here I am. Not quite as good as new, but at least, I'm still in one piece."

I covered her hand with mine. "What an awful thing. Thank God you're ok."

"Yes, I was lucky. But I still have some pain. It's manageable. Most of the time, an over-the-counter pill does the trick. I don't want to become dependent on prescription drugs. Especially because of...."

Finally, Neecy said, "I'm not sure you know about this, Carol. But our only son, Anthony, died of a drug overdose right before he graduated from high school." Her eyes were filled with tears, and who could blame her?

Her voice trailed off, and for once I kept my mouth shut. But I covered her hand with mine and held it tightly.

Neecy sighed deeply and squeezed my hand. "Thanks, Carol. It's still very hard."

Porter must have sensed her mistress's mood, because she raced across the yard and plopped down at Neecy's feet. Dogs can be very intuitive to people that they love.

"Tony gave Porter to me to help me recover from the accident," Neecy said, stroking her dog's head. "I don't know what I would do without her. And you know how demanding a puppy can be. She had to be walked, and fed, and generally taken care of. She was the best medicine I could have had. Having to take care of her forced me to get back on my feet."

"Dogs are wonderful therapy," I said. "And Tony sounds like a dream husband."

"He is most of the time," Neecy said. "But now that I'm better, I want to do more things for myself. Tony means well, but he doesn't seem to understand that. And I'm betting that he'll want me to get more involved in his campaign. It's not that I want him to lose, but I'm basically a shy person. Talking to strangers at cocktail parties is not my idea of a good time."

I didn't want to learn anymore intimate information about Neecy and Tony's marriage. I have enough trouble trying to figure out my own relationship sometimes. So I changed the subject.

"I bet Meg was helpful while you were recovering from your accident," I said. "I know that having close friends around whenever I've gone through a rough time has been invaluable for me."

Ok, I was fishing for information here. So sue me. I bet you're curious, too.

"You're kidding again, right, Carol? Meg rarely thinks about anybody but herself. And until she showed up on my doorstep three weeks ago, I hadn't seen her for years."

I couldn't wait to e-mail Nancy with what I'd found out.

I thought the reunion meeting went well today, and hope your house showing did, too. Meg storming out was a blessing. Maybe she'll make good on her threat and boycott the reunion, too. Neecy stayed here later and her dog, Porter, and Lucy and Ethel got along great. I was surprised. You'd have thought they were old friends, the way they were running around the yard together. Yes, even Lucy! And you won't believe this. Neecy told me that she hadn't seen Meg in years. She said Meg just showed up on her doorstep three weeks ago. How about that! And how the heck did you find her? Do you know what dear Meg has been doing all these years? She was nosy enough about all of our lives, but kept mum about what she'd been up to. What do you think? And more importantly, WHAT DO YOU KNOW? *And you better share! Love, C*

Nancy's reply was instantaneous .

I did know Meg hadn't seen Neecy in years. I called Neecy when I was trying to track Meg down, among others in their crowd. I guess I forgot to tell you that. I can't remember how I found her. It could have been through Facebook. Anyway, she's the same control freak she always was, and I'm glad she stormed out of the meeting, too. Her idea of a pole dancing class was disgusting. I hope she crawls back under whatever rock she was hiding under, and stays there. Gotta go. Big date tonight with You Know Who. Love you back. N

"That Nancy," I said to Ethel. "She doesn't mince words about anyone, especially someone she can't stand."

Unlike me, who tries to find something good in everyone. But I don't want to brag.

"Where's Meg been for almost forty years?" I asked the dogs. "And what's she been doing? And why didn't she want to talk about herself? Heaven knows, when we were in high school, that's all she did."

"You're talking to yourself again, Carol," said Jim, who'd walked into the office in time to hear the last part of my one-way conversation. "And what's this about Meg?"

"In the first place, *dear,* I was not talking to myself," I said with the assurance of someone who knows she's been caught doing something really stupid by someone who'd never, under any circumstances, understand why. But I made a vain attempt to explain myself, anyway.

"I was talking to Lucy and Ethel. They're very good listeners. Non-judgmental. Non-critical. And they never answer me back.

"Plus, they have perfect, consistent hearing. Unlike other beings who reside in this house and whose hearing is selective, to say the least."

Jim gave me a dirty look. The kind he always gives me when he's on the defensive. "Don't try and change the subject, Carol. And never mind who you were talking to. What do you know about Meg?"

"Nothing, Jim," I said slowly. "Nothing at all. How does a person drop out of sight for almost forty years? And, more importantly, why?"

Chapter 19

The secret to staying young is to live honestly, eat slowly, and drink in moderation. Now, I ask you, what kind of fun is that?

Once Meg vanished from the reunion committee and, hopefully, from Fairport as well, I didn't obsess about her anymore. She was gone, and that was that.

Besides, we only had a few months to plan what Nancy insisted on calling our Ruby Reunion. The way she was pushing the rest of the committee around and giving us a dizzying array of assignments, some people started calling her Captain Bligh behind her back.

I'll confess that privately I agreed with their assessment of Nancy's high-handed organizing techniques. But as her very best friend, I felt obligated to defend her behavior by reminding everyone, including Claire – who was always the most vocal critic – that Terry, Nancy's only daughter, was away in the Peace Corps and only heaven knew if or when she'd ever come home. Nancy would probably never get the chance to help organize any important events in Terry's life. Like her wedding, for example. So throwing herself into the reunion planning was perfectly understandable.

Belatedly, I remembered how I had resisted Nancy's attempt to help me organize Jenny and Mark's wedding last December. Instead, Jim and I hired a professional wedding planner, and things didn't exactly go as planned for anyone.

Especially the wedding planner.

So what if Nancy was a little over the top about this reunion? Forgive, forget and move on. That's what I always say.

Well, that's sometimes what I say. And every once in a while, I mean it, too.

"I've had the most terrific idea," Nancy said at what I fervently hoped was our last reunion planning meeting. Honestly, organizing this reunion was taking up more time than planning a presidential summit.

Not that I know that from personal experience, you understand. But I bet I'm right. Plus, the President has a staff to organize that sort of thing. We were just a handful of (late) middle-aged women with children. Husbands. Dogs. In other words, responsibilities. And lives that did not live, eat and breathe for this reunion.

I hope I've made my point.

"Nancy, I swear, if you have one more terrific idea, I'll scream," Claire said. "And it's only two weeks until the reunion. We don't have time to add one more thing to the agenda."

Nancy chose to ignore Claire's outburst. "Things are coming together very nicely. I knew using that template from *High School Reunions For Dummies* would help us. And the staff at Dockside Living is doing a fantastic job converting our school to a senior living facility, too.

"What did I say that was so funny?"

The rest of us had doubled over laughing at Nancy's unintentional use of the word "converting." Hey, it's a Catholic thing. Saving pagan babies and all that stuff.

Never mind.

Nancy finally got the joke. "You're all terrible," she said. "Now, let's get back to business."

"Having Neecy on the reunion committee certainly made the building project hum right along. There's nothing like having the boss's wife involved to make things happen," Claire said.

"It's too bad she had to resign from our committee," Mary Alice said. "But when Tony officially announced his run for state senate, he asked her to limit her other commitments and devote her time to helping get him elected."

"Do you think Tony has a real chance of winning?" Mary Catherine asked. "His opponent is the incumbent, and from what I've read, he has the advantage."

"Tony Prentiss is one of the most determined men in town," Claire said. "Look at how he built his business up from nothing, and how successful he's become. And Larry says that making prescription drug abuse a cornerstone of Tony's campaign is giving him a load of positive publicity. It's such a huge problem all over the state, even in towns like Fairport. Whether the media attention will translate to actual votes, well, we'll find that out in November."

"Do you know that Tony and Neecy's only son died of a prescription drug overdose in high school?" Mary Beth asked. "It was a terrible time for them. Mary Ann, Mary Catherine and I did our best to help the family, but I can't imagine how someone gets over losing a child like that."

"This is Tony's way of fighting back against drug abuse, I guess," Mary Alice said. "And honoring the memory of their son. I can see why Neecy would want to help."

"I can, too," I said. And I realized how lucky Jim and I were, to have two wonderful children who still wanted us to be an important part of their lives.

"Let's go over the final spreadsheet for the reunion one more time," Nancy said.

There was a chorus of groans from the rest of us.

"Nancy," Claire objected, "we've been over this thing a million times. We have the catering completely under control. Saturday night will be at Maria's Trattoria, so you know everything will be perfect. The caterer at the school has designed a wonderful menu. It's low fat, but doesn't look or taste like it. Everyone will love it. The decorations are fantastic – and the tablecloths are ruby red, just like you wanted. The nametags are being made as soon as people respond. We already have enough people who've paid in advance that we're in the black."

Claire gave Nancy a cheeky grin. "I assume the budget is the one thing you didn't want to have in the red."

"Very funny," Nancy said.

"We also have the souvenir goody bags already prepared, thanks to Mary Catherine and Mary Ann," Claire continued, looking at the spreadsheet and ticking off each item in turn. "The contact list is up to date as of now. We may get some more information before the reunion, so it won't be printed until two days before the event, right, Mary Alice?"

She nodded. "The list is all laid out and we're ready to go. It's fantastic how many of the class we've been able to locate. Sister Rose was a wonderful help with that part."

"Don't forget how many people I'd already found thanks to the Realtors network," Nancy reminded us.

"Did we ever make a decision about the baby pictures?" Mary Beth asked. We all groaned again. One of the most stupid ideas Nancy had gleaned from *High School Reunions for Dummies* was to ask all our classmates, even the ones who weren't able to come to the actual reunion, to submit a baby picture of themselves. The idea was to put them all on a bulletin board at the check-in table and have people try to identify each infant.

"Good lord," I said, "I thought we shot down that idea a few weeks ago. We're not going to do that, are we? And it's two weeks before the reunion. I think it's too late to ask people."

"Not with the magic of e-mail," Nancy said. "We can still send out a blast and see how many people want to do it."

"Oh, puhleeze, no," I begged. "We agreed not to do it. We voted not to do it, for heaven's sake."

"Oh, all right," Nancy said. "We won't do it. But what about the awards? Mary Beth, do you have those under control?"

Mary Beth nodded. "I've made certificates for the classmate who traveled the farthest to get to the reunion, who has the most children and grandchildren, and who's been married the longest. Did I forget anything?"

"I thought we were going to give an award for the person who's been married the most times," I said with a straight face.

"Oh, for heaven's sake," said Nancy. "That's just ridiculous."

"No," Claire said. "I love that idea. Think of the fun we'd have with that award."

Nancy huffed. "Let's wait another week before we make that decision."

"So should I make up a certificate for that category?" asked Mary Beth.

"Oh, what the hell. Go ahead," said our esteemed chairperson. "And now, it's time for my terrific idea. Are you ready?"

We weren't, but I knew from personal experience that Nancy was on a roll and there was no stopping her. And I was very afraid of that look in her eye. I'd seen that look before. It always got me into trouble, even when we were kids.

"I think we should stay overnight at Mount Saint Francis the night before the reunion. After all, we'll be exhausted from the party at Maria's Trattoria, and we have to be at school early Sunday to set up for the lunch. Isn't that a great idea?"

Nancy was bouncing in her seat, she was so excited.

Good grief. I couldn't imagine anything worse. I knew I'd never sleep, and if I did, I'd have nightmares.

But instead, I said, "Ok, I'm in. Sounds like fun."

I am truly a glutton for punishment.

Chapter 20

I believe in planning ahead. I've already told my family that, at my funeral, I want a 21-nun salute.

Less than one week remained until the reunion. So much left to do, and so little time to get it all done.

Or so I tried to explain to Jim on the Sunday morning before the Saturday night get-together at Maria's Trattoria. To which he was not invited, since the committee (that would be Nancy) decided that Significant Others of any persuasion would cramp our bonding potential.

Jim was not at all pleased at being left out of the party, despite the fact that I pointed out to him, in my most reasonable tone, that he and I didn't meet until college, and the only people he really knew from my high school class were Nancy, Claire and Mary Alice. All of whom he saw on a regular basis.

You'll notice I left Meg off the list. Hey, I'm not completely crazy, and besides, she hadn't bothered to send in a response so we were assuming she wouldn't show up.

What a shame. She certainly would be missed.

Not.

Jim laid his CVS pharmacy weekly sale flyer beside him on the kitchen table. Which meant that he had something *really* important to talk to me about. Because he treasures that weekly flyer more than a first edition of the Guttenberg Bible.

"Carol, I'm not trying to horn in on your fun," he said in a reasonable tone. "And I wouldn't even stay for the meal. I'd just like to poke my head inside the restaurant and see if I recognize anyone from the old days. I don't see anything wrong with that. What's the big deal?"

"The big deal, dear," I replied, "is that nobody else's significant other is doing that. Because the committee voted unanimously not to allow it. And, as you may recall, Mount Saint Francis Academy was an all-girls' school. I think you'd be noticed."

"Humph," Jim grumped. "I still don't see what the big deal is."

"Neither do I, dear," I said, trying to pacify him. "But that's the way it is. And there's nothing you or I can do about it."

Honestly, the whole situation was pretty comical. Because I was sure that if I'd asked Jim to come to the party, he would have told me, "No way. I don't want to be stuck in a room of post-menopausal women who are gabbing about their glorious high school days. Forget it. I won't go."

What is it about boys that, when you say no to something, that thing becomes even more attractive? Oh well.

Then I had a brilliant idea. A compromise. The kind of thing that long-term marriages are built on.

"How about this?" I said. "I'm going to be staying overnight at school after the party, and it's silly to bring my car when Nancy, Mary Alice and Claire will be driving theirs, too. Why don't you drop me off at Maria's Trattoria? And if you should just happen to walk by Maria's private dining room when the party is going on, and sneak a peek into the room, well, there's nothing anyone can say about that, right? What do you say?

"But you have to be discreet," I warned him. "And you have to get out of there before Nancy spots you."

"I'll think about it, Carol. Maybe I will. But it might not be worth it, after all. I probably won't know anybody. Maybe I'll call Larry and see if he wants to take in a movie instead."

And he left the kitchen, whistling.

I realized I'd just been snookered. All Jim wanted was an invitation so he could turn it down.

Men!

"You have to make me blond and beautiful by Saturday," I said to Deanna, proprietor of Fairport's leading hair salon, Crimpers, and my own personal lustrous locks magician. "I want a completely new hairstyle. And if you could figure out a way for me to lose ten pounds in the next few days, that'd be a bonus. It's my fortieth high school reunion this weekend, and I've got to be dazzling."

I plunked myself down in Deanna's chair. There was only one other customer in the salon, and she was under the dryer getting blasted with hot air. So I was able to speak freely without worrying about being overheard.

Deanna regarded me with a certain amount of annoyance. "Just out of curiosity, Carol, why did you wait until almost the very last minute to come in and want a makeover? I'm not a miracle worker, you know. Just a hard-working, underpaid hair stylist."

I was properly chastised. And chagrined. "You're absolutely right. I should have planned ahead more. Is it too late to do something a little different? It's really important to me."

"We could shave your head," Deanna said, grabbing some electric clippers and coming in my direction. "That'd be a real conversation starter."

I attempted to throw a towel at her. And missed, as usual.

"I know you're just kidding, Deanna. You are, right?"

Deanna laughed. "Of course I am, Carol. But I get pretty annoyed at people who come into the salon, especially brand new customers, and expect miracles. For you, though, I'll make the effort. But only with your hair. As far as losing ten pounds goes, you're on your own. Go put on a smock and let me get to work."

For the next half hour, Deanna concentrated on doing my color while I bored her with the details of the upcoming Ruby Reunion. Fortunately, she didn't nod off while she was putting foils in my hair.

"Ok, time for you to sit under the dryer for a bit," she said, leading me to a nearby chair and handing me some magazines to pass the time while she finished up her other client. I settled down to read some trashy magazines that I would never even glance at when I'm standing in line at the supermarket checkout counter.

Honest.

I started by skimming an issue of *Yelp!,* a magazine not known for challenging its readers' brain cells. I found myself drawn to a full-page advertisement for a brand new book.

"Forget *50 Shades of Grey!*" the teaser proclaimed. "Check out *50 Shades of Navy: Memories of a Catholic Girlhood.* Coming this month from Tell-All Books to a retail store near you. Also available as an e-book. Learn new and very creative ways to use knee socks! Hint: They're not just to keep your tootsies warm. For pre-publication ordering information, check our website, www.50shadesofnavy.com."

I checked the magazine publication date. Yikes! It was the October issue. That meant *50 Shades of Navy* would be released at exactly the same time as our high school reunion was being held.

And you'll never guess what Nancy had decided to put in all the goody bags. Ruby red knee socks with our school logo on them.

Chapter 21

I'm in the initial stage of my golden years:
AARP, SS, and IRAs.

"Fifty shades of navy?" Sister Rose asked. "I never realized there were so many. Here, Carol," she said, leading me over to a rack of blazers, "take a look at these." And she pulled four or five jackets out for my inspection. "Perhaps one of these might work with whatever it is you're trying to match." Then she frowned. "But if there are fifty shades to choose from, you'd better bring in your slacks or skirt to be sure it really matches a blazer or a sweater. The eye can be so deceiving. Are you looking for something to wear for the reunion? "

I gave Sister Rose a questioning look. Because I wasn't sure if she was putting me on or not.

I'd gone to Sally's Closet, to give her a head's up about the hot book being released this month. And instead of reacting as I'd expected – that would be shock, horror, etc. like any other normal nun would – she was giving me a fashion lesson.

Good grief.

"Thanks, Sister," I said, handing her back the jackets she'd selected for me. "But the fifty shades of navy I'm talking about have nothing to do with fashion choices."

I paused, not exactly sure how to proceed. How does one discuss a book like this one with a Catholic nun? No class in high school – or college, either, for that matter – included tips on handling this kind of situation.

I took a good look at Sister Rose and realized that she was pressing her lips together tightly. I wasn't sure how to read that. Disapproval? Annoyance? Impatience that I hadn't bought one of the darned navy blue blazers to wear to the reunion?

"Good gracious, Carol," Sister said, "do you think I've been living under a rock for the past year or so? I've heard of *Fifty Shades of Grey*. Disgusting. And the fact that people are paying good money to buy that filth, well, words fail me."

Not for long, of course.

Sister took the navy blazers and rehung them in the proper size classifications. Slammed them into their proper sizes, in fact. I felt sorry for the blazers, but better them than me.

"And, yes, I know about this new piece of filth, too," she said, emphasizing the word *filth*. "I see no need to talk about it, with you or anyone else. It's just some person trying to capitalize on the success of what is basically a pornographic book. Making up titillating stories about her Catholic adolescence to sell her own book. Disgraceful. Nobody is going to buy it."

"Sister, with all due respect, I think people are going to buy it," I responded. "Not me, of course," I added to diffuse Sister's shocked look. "I agree with you that it is filth. But what if the book is about a school for girls and people think it's Mount Saint Francis? It could impact our entire reunion."

"That is complete rubbish, Carol," Sister Rose said with such vehemence that she made me cringe. Just like the bad old days. "You're anticipating a problem where none exists. And for your information, the publisher had the nerve to send me an advance reader copy of this book and ask me for a comment. So I know what I'm talking about."

"You have a copy of *Fifty Shades of Navy?*" I asked, to be sure I'd heard correctly. "I can't believe it."

I resisted the urge to ask her if I could take a quick peek.

"I don't have it anymore, Carol," Sister Rose said. "Once I realized what the book was about, I threw it right in the garbage. Which is exactly where it belongs. Now, please excuse me. I have extra work to do today. We're short on volunteers."

She gave me a hard look, which I read loud and clear. Note to self: Either avoid the thrift shop entirely or get back on a regular volunteer schedule pronto.

"I'll see you Saturday night at Maria's Trattoria for the welcome cocktail party," Sister Rose said, indicating that the subject of *Fifty Shades of Navy* was closed. And not likely to be reopened anytime soon. Like, never.

I started to respond that I might be able to lend a hand in the shop for an hour or so (Catholic guilt – I'll never get over it), but Sister Rose didn't give me a chance. In fact, the good sister made such a hasty exit that she almost collided with a volunteer who was on her way into the shop with a cart full of donations.

"Sorry, Sister Rose," said the volunteer, immediately assuming the blame for the near collision. "I didn't see you."

"Not a problem," said Sister, disappearing through the door and closing it firmly behind her.

Hmm. That was weird. Sister Rose ran away from me as quickly as I tried to run away from her in junior year. Before I could pin her down and ask her more questions. I wondered how she managed that feat. I never could.

Well, if Sister Rose wasn't worried about *Fifty Shades of Navy* ruining our fortieth class reunion, why the heck should I?

Because usually, when you jump to conclusions, like you're doing right now, it turns out that you're right.

"Earth to Carol," said the volunteer, bringing me back to the current century with a thud. "It's me, Mary Beth. Or, if Sister Rose is listening, it's *I*, Mary Beth. She always was such a stickler for grammar. Remember?

What the heck was that all about? I've never seen her move that fast in the thrift shop."

I laughed, gave my classmate a big hug, and ignored her question. "I didn't know you volunteered here, Mary Beth. It's good to see you." I turned my attention to the cart she was pushing. "What kind of goodies do you have? Anything we can use to decorate tables for the reunion this weekend?"

"Hardly," Mary Beth said. "To tell you the truth, the donations have been down the last few months. I think that, with the economy so bad, more people are consigning things to make a little extra cash than donating them here for a tax deduction. I worry sometimes that we'll eventually have to close the thrift shop, and that'll mean cutting off a major revenue stream for the domestic violence program."

"How long have you been volunteering here, Mary Beth?" I asked, picking up a crystal candy dish and holding it up to the light. "This is pretty." I set it back down on the cart and sighed. "But I don't need to add one more thing to my house. I'm trying to pare my inventory down. At least, that's what I tell my husband."

Mary Beth took the candy dish and placed it on a shelf in the window so it could sparkle and, hopefully, catch a customer's eye. "I've been here about six months," she said. "I wandered in here one day to kill a little time while I was waiting for a train to the city. As many times as I'd been to the train station, I never noticed this shop before. And Sister Rose swooped in and cornered me."

She shrugged. "The rest, as the saying goes, is history. Who can say no to Sister Rose? Certainly not me."

I laughed. "She got me exactly the same way," I said. "Although, I have to confess that I haven't been in to volunteer for several months. As Sister Rose just reminded me in her own, not-so-subtle way. My daughter was married recently, and I was involved in planning the wedding. Time just got away from me."

Ok, some of you know that I wasn't *that* involved in planning Jenny's wedding. But I was involved in several things that revolved around the wedding. And as the mother of the (recent) bride, I'm entitled to stretch the truth when I feel the need.

"Here, let me give you a hand," I said to Mary Beth. "I have a little time to spare before I have to get home. I'm not going in the back to put on a volunteer apron, though. I'm not a complete idiot."

Mary Beth laughed. "You mean you don't want a chance to continue your conversation with Sister Rose," she said, giving me some linens and directing me to fold them and put them on their proper shelves. "We like to separate everything, to make it easier for customers to find what they're looking for," she explained to me. "Although, by the end of the day, everything is usually all mixed up."

"Like I am at the end of a day," I said. "At least, that's what my family says."

Mary Beth laughed. "I know exactly what you mean."

"You know," I continued as I struggled to fold a contour bedsheet, "I'm really glad that you joined our reunion committee. You and Mary Catherine and Mary Ann. I finally figured out who's who."

"It's been such fun getting reacquainted," Mary Beth said. "Or maybe, as far as you and I are concerned, I should say that it's been such fun getting acquainted in the first place. Since we were never that friendly in high school."

"I wonder why that was," I said. "Honestly, I have no idea."

"You were so involved with the school newspaper, and so important in high school, that I figured you didn't have time for someone like me," Mary Beth said.

"You're kidding," I said. "I was the most insecure person in our class."

"No way," Mary Beth retorted. "That honor is all mine."

She turned away and busied herself with some towels for a minute. "I never told you this," she finally said, turning to face me again. "But I was jealous of you."

"What? Jealous of me? Why? For what?" I was truly amazed at this revelation from my classmate.

"I envied your ability to write," Mary Beth said. "And have things published in the school paper. Your columns were so witty. I don't know how you did it. I always wanted to write. But, like a lot of the other girls in our class, the most I ever wrote was jottings in a notebook. And they were pretty pathetic." She colored slightly. "Ridiculous stuff, really."

"We all did that," I said. "I wrote in my diary every single night before I went to sleep. I looked at it a while ago and realized it was filled with really boring stuff. If my kids ever saw it, they'd think I had no life. And, come to think of it, I guess I didn't."

We both laughed.

"So, what were you and Sister Rose talking about before she took off for the back room of the shop?" Mary Beth asked. "Like I said, I've never seen her move so fast. Except when she has to get to a meeting with a prospective donor."

Careful, Carol. Mary Beth doesn't need to know about Fifty Shades of Navy. *And no one else in our class does, either. At least, not from you.*

"Oh, we were just having a discussion about final arrangements for the reunion," I said, not looking at Mary Beth directly. "Sister Rose wanted nametags for the cocktail party, and I reminded her that the committee had already nixed that idea."

I sensed that Mary Beth knew I wasn't telling her the truth, but she'd decided to let the matter drop.

And later, during reunion weekend, I really wished she hadn't.

Chapter 22

I'm so old I don't even buy green bananas.

The brilliant October sunshine streaming in my bedroom window forced me to open my eyes and focus. Unfortunately, despite the fact that I had yet to don my specs, I focused on the fact that my bedroom window was streaked with the remnants of a recent rainstorm. Which was magnified by the brilliant sun.

Yuck. Add washing windows to my ever growing list of household chores to avoid as long as possible.

Hmm. On second thought, maybe I could pass this one over to Jim. He'd become my little helper ever since his retirement, often eclipsing me in household duties. Taking some of them over completely, to tell the truth.

Of course, he doesn't do them nearly as well as I do. Not that I'd tell him that.

I squinted at the clock and realized it was almost eight. Wow. I hadn't slept this late in a long time. And I realized that I didn't even hear Jim get up. Again.

I rolled over in my nice warm bed and right on top of Lucy, who made it crystal clear with a low growl that I'd intruded on her personal space. "Sorry, Luce," I said. "I didn't know you were there. And where's Ethel?"

I attempted to put my feet on the hardwood floor next to the bed and, instead, encountered the other Andrews canine, snoring gently in a patch of sunlight. With a scribbled note attached to her collar.

It's going to be a helluva reunion. I'd crash the whole thing, if I thought I could pass as a female. Turn on Channel 9. Love, Jim.

I reached for the remote on the bedside table and turned the television on to Channel 9, as Jim had suggested. I was just starting to focus on the interview, which consisted of Marni Barker, *Wake Up New England*'s cheery co-host, talking to someone who was inexplicably hiding behind a screen, when my cell phone beeped, indicating an incoming text. Then another beep. And another.

Holy cow. What was going on?

Then, the house phone rang. I picked it up to hear Nancy screeching in my ear. "Good God, Carol. Did you see the story on *Wake Up New England* this morning? A horrible book, *Fifty Shades of Navy,* was released today and everyone will think it's about us! The reunion will be a disaster. We'll have to cancel. Or be the laughing stock of Fairport. Say something, Carol. Are you there? Do you hear me?"

I looked at the clock again. It was only ten minutes after eight. I hadn't even gotten out of bed yet. I wanted to brush my teeth, wash my face and perform my other usual morning ablutions.

And, most of all, I wanted coffee. Lots and lots of coffee. I wondered if it was too early to add some brandy to it.

Heck, it had to be five o'clock somewhere.

"It's too late to cancel," Claire said. "And why should we? This book has nothing to do with Mount Saint Francis Academy, or any of us." She looked around at the rest of the reunion committee huddled around my dining room table. "Unless someone here has a secret life. Anyone want to 'fess up?"

"Claire's right," Mary Catherine said. Usually the most timid member of the committee, we were all startled to hear her voice an opinion. Heck, we were all startled to hear her voice, period.

"I think it's just a coincidence that the book is being released the same weekend as our reunion," I said with more confidence than I felt. "I bet there are hundreds of other reunions going on all over the country this weekend. And a good percentage of them are for graduates of high schools just like ours." I trained my sights on our jittery leader. "Nancy, you're completely overreacting here."

Overreacting is something I'm always accused of by my nearest and dearest, so I knew what I was talking about. And the accusations against moi were unjustifiable and untrue, in case you were wondering.

Nancy's face flushed dark crimson. She does not like to be criticized, in public or in private. Another behavior pattern I can completely identify with.

We were diverted from additional conversation by the sound of my front doorbell. Thank the Good Lord. And I knew who it was. The one person who could make some sense out of this very disturbing situation.

"Sister Rose is here," I announced, leading her back into my dining room with as much speed as I could get away with and still be polite. "I thought it would be good to invite her to this meeting. To calm everyone down and put things in the proper perspective."

I hope.

"So, Sister," I said, pulling out a chair and gesturing her to sit, "can I get you anything? Coffee? Tea? A soft drink?"

"Thank you, but no, Carol," Sister Rose said. "I'm too upset. I saw *Wake Up New England* this morning. I'm sure all of you did, too. About that terrible book, *Fifty Shades of Navy.* What a disgrace, to give that kind of filth major publicity."

"We were just talking about the book, Sister," I said. "And whether we should cancel our reunion. What do you think? You have to admit that the timing is pretty bad."

"I see no reason to cancel the reunion," Sister Rose said. "But that's really up to all of you. You're the committee, after all. I'm merely an advisor."

Yeah, right. If it weren't for you, we wouldn't be doing this stupid reunion in the first place. Are you conveniently forgetting this was partly your idea?

I didn't really say that, of course.

"At this late date, I don't see how the reunion could be cancelled," Sister Rose continued, in case she hadn't made her point crystal clear. "I understand that there are classmates coming in from all over New England. Am I right?" she addressed Mary Ann, the keeper of the official attendance list, who nodded in agreement.

"That's exactly what I was just saying, Sister," said Claire. "And I still don't see what everyone is getting so excited about. It's just a novel."

Sister Rose took a deep breath. "That's because none of you have seen *Fifty Shades of Navy*. Unfortunately, I have. The publisher had the gall to send me an advance reader copy and ask me for a comment."

"Who is the publisher?" Mary Alice asked. "And how did the company get your name and contact information?"

"Exactly what I was wondering," said Sister Rose. "The publishing company is called Tell-All Books." She sniffed her disapproval. "I'd never heard of them before. Last week, the book arrived, Priority Mail, with a return address of a post office box on Long Island. There was a brief cover letter on cheap stationary asking me to read the book and submit a comment for review. When I read the back cover description, I was shocked."

Her voice trembled. "I'm not used to seeing books like that. It's nothing but cheap trash. And how the publisher had the nerve to contact me, well, I was completely disgusted. And angry. I threw the book in the garbage before anyone else could see it."

"Sister Rose, with all due respect," I said, "perhaps it would have been better if you hadn't thrown the book away. I understand how shocked you must have been to get the book in the first place. But maybe there was a way to contact the publisher, or the author. Wouldn't you like to know how they got your name?"

"I am not a complete idiot, Carol," Sister Rose retorted. "Of course I wanted to know why I was contacted."

I sat back in my chair, in my own dining room, in my own house, and felt like I was fourteen years old again.

Sister Rose saw my reaction and said, "Oh, Carol, I'm sorry to take my frustration out on you. I'm just so upset."

I responded with a quick nod. And hoped none of the rest of the committee had noticed that my eyes were threatening to spill over onto my best white linen tablecloth.

"I went on the computer," Sister Rose continued, "and found a website for the book, which has the same contact information as Tell-All Books. I sent an e-mail, demanding answers. And got no response. None."

Hmm. Now, that was interesting. At the risk of being shot down once again, I said, "It's pretty easy to get a book published these days. Sometimes, the author is also the publisher. I wonder if that's what happened here."

At that moment, my cell phone chirped, indicating an incoming message. "Sorry, everybody," I said. "I thought I turned the phone off."

Then I looked at the message and realized that it was a text from my darling son, Mike. Since his communications to Jim and me have been slim to none for the past few months, there was no way I was going to ignore that text. No matter now rude that appeared to everyone else.

"Excuse me," I said to the group. "This is from my son. It may be important. I have to read it right away."

"How about if I make another pot of coffee while you're doing that?" Claire suggested. "I don't know about the rest of you, but a shot of some fresh caffeine may help me think clearer."

"I'll help you," said Mary Alice, jumping up to clear a few dirty dishes from the table and follow Claire into my kitchen.

"Thanks," I said, so distracted by the message from Mike that I had to read it several times before I understood it.

Hey, Cosmo girl! Check out this link: http://fiftyshadesofnavy.youtube.com/watch. You're famous!

At first, I was hesitant to click on the link, for fear it was a spam message. But then I realized that only Mike calls me Cosmo girl (a reference to my brief but brilliant copy editing career many years ago), so the text had to be legit.

The link led me to a one-minute book trailer hyping *Fifty Shades of Navy,* which was mainly a series of images flashing on the screen, one after the other, to a rock and roll song. I think the song was, "Only The Good Die Young." But I can't be sure.

Because one image, although a very quick one, was unmistakable. And it was cleverly inserted several times among the other, more titillating images. It was the front portico of Mount Saint Francis Academy.

Chapter 23

I got great news at the supermarket the other day. Campbell's alphabet soup now comes in a large type version.

I got up so quickly I tipped my chair over onto the dining room floor.

"Everybody up," I said, ignoring my clumsiness. "And follow me into the office, where we can check out this YouTube link that Mike's sent me. Now."

"What's the matter with you, Carol?" asked Nancy. "You're acting crazy. And your face is as white as a sheet."

"No questions. Just come on," I urged my classmates. "You'll soon see why."

Fortunately, Jim had left the computer on after he checked the credit card balances this morning. (I do what I can to support the economy. I feel it's my duty as a United States citizen, not that Jim goes along with that argument for a single second.)

In no time at all, with everyone, even Claire and Mary Alice, crowded around my computer, I entered the link that Mike had sent and there it was: the book trailer from hell.

And irrefutable proof that, whoever the mysterious author of this book was, she had to be an alumna of Mount Saint Francis Academy. The chances of our high school portico being chosen at random for the book trailer, from among thousands of other schools nationwide, was impossible.

"I can't believe it," Sister Rose said. "This makes Mount Saint Francis Academy look like a training school for...ladies of the evening."

One of our group tittered. I was afraid to look around and see who it was. But then, I hear someone else laugh. A little louder, this time.

And before I knew it, I heard more people laughing. Well, the whole situation was ridiculous. I tried to stop myself, but I couldn't. I began to giggle, myself.

"I fail to see the humor in this situation," Sister Rose said. Which made the rest of us laugh even louder.

"Oh, come on, Sister Rose," Claire said. "You really are funny. The idea of anyone thinking our high school was a training ground for hookers is absolutely hilarious. Nobody's going to believe that. Why, we even had to kneel to be sure our uniform skirts were long enough, remember? If they didn't touch the floor, we were sent home with a note."

"Well, at least we know how the publisher got your contact information, Sister," I said. "It looks like the mysterious author really is a Mount Saint Francis graduate."

"I wonder if she's a member of our class," Mary Alice said. "Wouldn't that be something? A celebrity classmate!"

"Hardly anything I would cheer about," Sister Rose said.

"Well, I, for one, am curious as to how she came up with the idea for a book like this in the first place," I said. "I know how much research Jim has to do when he's writing an article. I wonder if she did research, too. You know what I mean? Hands on."

That did it. Even Sister Rose managed a small smile at my joke, while the rest of us dissolved into howls of laughter.

"And, by the way," Nancy said, "none of us, except you, Sister, have even seen the book. So maybe the book is all flash and no substance, if you know what I mean. It could just be a huge publicity stunt."

Mary Catherine (remember her?) raised her hand. Just like she used to do in high school. "I saw the story about the book on *Wake Up New England,* too. I thought it was very strange that the author was being interviewed behind a privacy screen, so she wouldn't be identified. I tuned in at the middle of the interview, though, so I don't know if there was any explanation for that. But I thought that was very odd."

"You see!" said Nancy. "It's all just a huge publicity stunt to sell books. I knew it. Just give a book a suggestive title, add a little extra mystery with an author who remains anonymous, and the books will fly off the shelves. And whatever e-books fly off from."

I had to admit, that made some sense. As the wife of a former New York City public relations guru, I knew first-hand some of the crazy stunts PR agencies would do to gain publicity for a product. And, after all, a book is a product, just like laundry detergent or an automobile.

"You know," I said, with more enthusiasm than I thought I could muster up after viewing the book trailer, "I bet it's possible that someone could go on an Internet site like classmates.com and put in a date to find out when any school in the country was doing a reunion. And after that, schedule a book launch on that date, to make it look like the mysterious author was connected with that school. Maybe this is going on all over the country and we just don't know about it."

That made such good sense to me. And to the rest of the committee else as well. And, thank goodness, to Sister Rose.

Whew. I knew all those dinners where Jim shared his public relations war stories with Jenny, Mike and me would come in handy someday.

"All right, everybody," Nancy said, "are we in agreement that the Ruby Reunion will go on as scheduled, starting tomorrow night with the welcome cocktail party at Maria's Trattoria? All those in favor, say aye!"

Of course, it was unanimous. The show must go on. But we all decided to keep an extra close eye on our attendees. Just in case one of them dropped any subtle hints about pursuing a late-life writing career.

"This party will be just like an Agatha Christie mystery," Mary Alice said. "All the suspects will be in one place. And then Carol will figure out who the author is. Just like you've solved other mysteries in the past."

Modesty prevented me from agreeing with Mary Alice. And, also, I didn't have the faintest idea how I'd ferret out the culprit. But I did appreciate her faith in my detecting prowess.

"It's possible that the person who wrote *Fifty Shades of Navy* will be at our reunion," Sister Rose said. "I don't think the author would miss a chance to come back and see what kind of reaction her book is getting from her classmates, do you? Assuming, of course, that she is a member of your class."

"Everybody has to be on alert tomorrow night at the party," Nancy said. "Mingle with as many people as you can. If you find someone you think is suspicious, let me know right away."

I snapped a salute. "Yes, ma'am. Whatever you say, ma'am. But I still think this is just a publicity stunt, and we've got nothing to worry about."

And, well, let's just say I wouldn't be at all surprised if several reunion committee members ordered *Fifty Shades of Navy* as an e-book tonight. In case someone referenced something at the reunion that was a hint as to the author's identity.

Just like we used to cram for exams, way back when.

Remember, old habits die hard.

Chapter 24

Hello. I know you. Can you tell me your name?

"Wasn't the party at Maria's Trattoria terrific?" Nancy said. "All things considered, it was a perfect way to start off our fortieth reunion. And not one person mentioned that horrible book. Thank God. Everyone was too busy catching up after all these years. Of course, we're nowhere nearer figuring out the identity of the author."

"I'm sure this is all a publicity stunt," I said for the umpteenth time. "I bet other schools having reunions this weekend are sweating this out, just like we are. Forget about it. Everyone who RSVP'd to the reunion was at the party tonight. There were no surprises."

"And tomorrow's lunch will be even better," Nancy predicted as we drove through the night in the direction of Mount Saint Francis. "Especially after we get a good night's sleep at school. I can't believe we're really having a sleepover there. This is going to be so much fun."

Nancy checked the lighted dial of her watch. "We'd better get a move on, Carol, or everyone else will be there before we are." And with that announcement, she floored the car engine and we took off like a rocket.

I know I should be used to Nancy's driving by now, but her love of speed scares me. The only way I can deal with it without screaming my lungs out is to close my eyes and pray. Which I was now doing.

"It was a great party, Carol," Nancy repeated, oblivious to her now whimpering passenger. "And you were right about one thing. But by the time I realized it, the party was already going strong and there wasn't anything we could do. We'll have them for tomorrow's lunch, though."

"I love it when I'm right," I said through clenched teeth. "Be a pal and tell me what I was right about. And maybe you'd slow down, just a little bit, while you tell me. We don't want to get a speeding ticket on our way to school."

Nancy eased up on the accelerator. "Sorry. You're right. I have a lead foot sometimes. You were right about the nametags. We should have had them at the welcome party. There were several people at the party who knew me, but I had no idea who they were. And after exchanging hugs and air kisses, I was embarrassed to admit it."

"The same thing happened to me," I said. "It was extra confusing because the restaurant also had a wedding reception going on in the next room. I kept getting the people mixed up. I was having a lovely conversation with a woman who looked very familiar, and after a few minutes, I realized she wasn't in our class at all. She was the mother of the groom. Boy, did I feel stupid. But we both had a good laugh about it."

"It was great that Neecy stopped in," Nancy said. "Although she couldn't stay long. She said something about a campaign event she had to go to for her husband. Did you get to talk to her?"

"Just for a second," I said. "We're trying to arrange a play date for our dogs. She said she'll definitely be at the luncheon tomorrow."

Even in the darkness, I could see Nancy raise a perfectly arched eyebrow. "A play date for the dogs? What the heck are you talking about? That's just about the stupidest thing I've ever heard."

I opened my mouth to reply, but didn't get the chance.

"Oh, never mind about that now," my chauffeur said. "We're here." She rolled to a stop in front of the looming structure that was our old high school. "There're a few cars in the parking lot. I knew the rest of the committee would beat us here."

"It wasn't a race, Nancy," I said. "And as the chairman of the reunion, I figured you'd want to stay behind until everyone else left the welcome party."

Truthfully, I was glad the rest of the committee was at school ahead of us. Although I knew it was stupid, the thought of going into that building at night creeped me out.

"Do we have to ring the doorbell?" I asked, dragging my overnight bag up the steps to the main door. "At least the front light is on."

Nancy gave me a look. "You're kidding, right? There's a keypad next to the door. All we have to do is punch in the correct code and the door will open. You are so last century, Carol. You'd better get into the modern age."

Humph. I decided, in the interest of harmony between best friends, to let that remark pass. I hope you're all proud of me.

Nancy punched in seven numbers and the door clicked open. "Is this safe?" I asked as we walked into the lobby. "What if someone forgets the code and can't get inside? And what about security?"

"Fairport Manor will have twenty-four hour security once it's officially open," Nancy informed me. "There'll always be someone at the reception desk, too. In case of an emergency. And I'm sure every resident will be given some sort of alternate access method. In case there's a power failure, for instance, when the keypad isn't working. We'll probably find out all about that tomorrow, when our class has the grand tour."

I headed through the darkened lobby in the general direction of the marble staircase, lugging my suitcase in one hand and my purse in the other. Sheesh. What the heck did I pack in this thing? It weighed a ton.

"Come on, Carol," Nancy said, following close behind me. "Don't tell me you insist on using the stairs when there's a perfectly good elevator. You have more phobias than...well, you have a lot of phobias."

"Just remember that I agreed to stay overnight here because you talked me into it," I said. "I'd rather be home in my own bed, even if Jim would be snoring up a storm and keeping me awake. You told me this would be fun. When, exactly, does the fun start? I don't want to miss it."

"When you look back on this reunion, you'll be glad we stayed here overnight, Carol," Nancy said. "And I admit I talked you into it, so there. I hope you're satisfied. Let's not argue about this."

"We have a long day ahead of us tomorrow," I said. "Climbing the stairs will be good exercise. I don't know about you, but I had way too much food at the welcome party tonight. If you don't want to walk, though, that's fine with me. Take the elevator and I'll see you on the third floor."

"Oh, all right," Nancy grumbled. "Lead on."

"I can't believe our room is in the former cloister," I said. I was puffing a little from the stairs, but I wasn't going to admit that to Nancy. "Are Claire and Mary Alice next door to us? I like the idea of having all of us close together."

It's less freaky. Not that I would admit that.

"We're in three-one-eight," said Nancy, checking the key fob. "I think they're at the end of the hall." She put her hand over her heart and panted for dramatic effect. "I'm out of breath from climbing all those stairs. Here, you open the door,' she said, handing me the key.

When I touched the door, searching for the lock, it swung open. Unaided.

"That's odd," I said.

"Maybe the ghosts of nuns past got here ahead of us and staked out a claim," Nancy said.

"You are just hilarious," I said, fumbling on the wall for the light switch. In a flash (sorry about the pun) the room was bathed in light.

"Oh." I stopped short, and Nancy careened into me. "Are you sure this is the right room? There's someone asleep in one of the beds."

"Of course this is our room," Nancy huffed. She went outside and checked the number against the key, just to be sure.

"One of the other committee members must have gotten confused. I don't want to scare her, but we have to wake her up. Otherwise, we'll have to find another room."

"Do you have any idea who it is?" I whispered.

"I have no idea," Nancy said. "Someone with white hair. That certainly narrows the possibilities down. And there's no need to whisper, Carol. Especially since we want her to wake up and leave. Why don't you see if you can rouse her?"

I gave Nancy a dirty look. "Why do I always have to do the hard jobs? Thanks a lot."

I crossed the room and touched the sleeping woman's arm. Gently. I didn't want to scare her.

"Excuse me," I said in a low voice. "I'm sorry to wake you, but you're in the wrong room. "

"Goodness, she certainly is a sound sleeper," Nancy said. "She didn't even move."

I touched the woman's arm again.

Nothing. No response.

Oh, lord.

"Nancy," I said, "we have to get out of here. Right now."

I pushed her out the door. "Is your phone in your pocket? Mine's packed in my suitcase."

"What?"

"Just give it to me!" I reached out my hand and snatched the phone. I was trembling all over.

"What in the world are you talking about, Carol? It's so late. Who on earth do you want to call at this hour?"

"The police. The woman in our room isn't sleeping. She's dead."

Chapter 25

My husband is retired. He was tired yesterday, and he's even more tired today.

Looking back on that night after a few weeks had passed, I had to admit that I was proud of the way I handled discovering the dead body at our reunion weekend. There may be some of you who recall a few other times – two, in fact – when I'd been faced with a similar situation. I'm not counting the first time I got involved with a dead body, since Jim deserves the honors on that occasion.

All of these, mind you, have happened since Jim retired. Do you think there could be a connection?

Maybe we need to get another hobby.

Anyway, on the previous two times I'd been personally involved in discovering a dead body, I'd reacted by dissolving into hysterical crying and/or screaming my lungs out for help.

But not this time. No sirree. Truth to tell, I was probably in total shock. But maybe I was also getting used to this sort of thing. Not to the point where I was immune to the horror of it. Or actually enjoying it. But I was calm. Even when I made the call to the Fairport police to report a death, I didn't babble.

Just the facts, ma'am. That was me.

Nancy, of course, was hysterical enough for both of us. I dragged her out of what was supposed to be our temporary home-away-from-home and locked the bedroom door with the key. I wasn't taking any chances on contaminating what could be a crime scene.

Not that I thought it was, understand. It's just that I've learned that any unattended death is suspicious. And that's why I insisted we call the police.

"Oh, God, Carol," Nancy said, gulping and trying to get control of herself. Unsuccessfully. "The reunion is ruined. All our planning…who would have thought…it's just so horrible…."

It's certainly ruined for one of us. Permanently.

I didn't really say that. Of course.

Instead, best friend that I am, I said, "Nancy, sweetie, maybe it would be best if you went to Claire and Mary Alice's room until the police get here. You can calm down a little there. Do you know what number their room is?"

Nancy looked at me in horror. "I couldn't leave you, Carol. Not with…her in our room. Dead." And she collapsed into sobs again.

"What the heck is going on out here?" demanded Claire, heading toward us down the hallway with the determination of a pit bull. "Some of us are trying to sleep. Why are you two out here in the hall? Mary Alice and I tried to stay up and wait for you two to get here, but we were too tired."

She gave me a look that reminded me of my mother when I was late from a date. An unpleasant memory, to be sure.

"You were supposed to be here an hour ago, so we could have a glass of wine together and then go to bed," Claire said. "Where were you?"

Mary Alice, hard on Claire's heels, took one look at Nancy and me and smacked Claire on her head. (Gosh, I've always wanted to do that.)

"For heaven's sake, Claire, keep your voice down. Do you want to wake up everybody else? Take a look at them. It's obvious that they've had a terrible shock."

She put her arm around Nancy and said, "Come on, sweetie. Let's go back into your room and you can tell us what happened."

Nancy recoiled in shock. “Hell, no. There’s no way I’m going back in there.” Then, looking at me, “Tell them what happened, Carol. Tell them what we found when we opened the door to our room.”

“Yes, Mrs. Andrews,” said another voice. A male voice. One I had hoped to never hear again. “Why don’t you tell us what happened? And why you called the Fairport police tonight?”

Rats.

There’s a line in one of my all-time favorite movies, *Casablanca,* where bar owner Humphrey Bogart says about his lost love, Ingrid Bergman, “Of all the gin joints in all the towns in all the world, she walks into mine.”

That pretty much sums up how I felt when I turned to face the shortest detective on the Fairport police force. My son-in-law’s odious partner, Paul Wheeler. Fortunately, before I could open my mouth, I saw the Mark’s welcome face, right behind Paul.

Except that Mark didn’t look happy to see me. In fact, he looked downright angry.

“Ok, Carol, what happened this time?” Mark asked. “Not another corpse to add to your body count, I hope.”

I stiffened. Son-in-law or not, he had some nerve talking to me like that. Wait’ll the next time he needed some help from me.

Nancy, bless her interfering heart, jumped right into the conversation.

“Why, Mark, it’s not like we go looking for these things. Carol and I are here for our high school reunion. It’s tomorrow.”

“Actually,” I said, taking the conversation back and locking eyes with my son-in-law, “the reunion is today. It must be after midnight by now.

“Anyway, a few of us decided to stay overnight here, and when Nancy and I went into the room that had been assigned to us, we found a dead body in one of the beds. Which we did not put there. And immediately called the police. As any good citizen would do.”

I heard a gasp from Claire, or maybe it was from Mary Alice. I still had my baby blues trained on Mark.

Mark looked at his partner, who had kept uncharacteristically silent during this exchange. Then he sighed. "I was kidding, Carol. Not very professional of me. I'm sorry. But I didn't imagine that you'd really…"

He turned to Paul. "Let's check it out."

"We locked the room, Mark," I said, handing him the key. "Just to be on the safe side. I do know something about police procedure. More than I ever wanted to, in fact."

Mark nodded, and the two detectives disappeared into what was supposed to be the site of a fun sleepover party.

The ping of the elevator announced the arrival of other members of the Fairport police force, including a police photographer. Not a group I was particularly keen to join, despite my reputation for being extraordinarily curious.

Instead, I allowed Claire and Mary Alice to shepherd Nancy and me down the hall to their room. Wordlessly, they handed Nancy and me a small glass of now-warm white wine, and urged us to take a sip. Or two.

"Now, tell. What happened?" Claire asked.

The enormity of what Nancy and I had discovered suddenly hit me and I began to cry. Not hysterically, the way Nancy did a while ago in the hallway. Quietly. Because it was just so sad.

One of our classmates, someone of our own age, had died tonight. Here, at our old high school. Ok, it wasn't exactly our old high school anymore. But you know what I mean, right?

And it could have happened to any one of us. The dying, I mean. A cardiac incident, perhaps. Or a massive stroke. At a certain age, doctors warn about the signs of one of these coming on.

It could be someone on the committee, or a classmate who'd decided to arrive a day early at the reunion and stay overnight here. For old times' sake.

Maybe she was even at the welcome cocktail party at Maria's Trattoria. Maybe I'd talked to her and we shared stories about spouses, children, even grandchildren. (Not that I have any of the latter, as far as I know.)

It was just so tragic.

At that moment, for the first time ever, I felt old. Scared. I realized that my life could end in an instant. Poof. All over. No more Carol Andrews.

I never felt that vulnerable before. And mortal. (Not the sin kind, in case that reference confused you.)

And worried. Because, well, what comes next?

I gulped down the wine and held out my glass for more. "Just a little. Please. It may help me sleep. Assuming any of us get any sleep tonight."

"Not in that bed," Nancy said. "No way. Even if they sterilize the sheets."

Of course, she was right. But, well, that was kind of harsh, even for Nancy. I did agree with her, though. No way was I sleeping in that room tonight.

Mary Alice put her arms around me and I started to cry in earnest. "You and Nancy can bunk in with us," she said. "We'll figure something out."

At that moment, just when I was starting to feel a little better, my son-in-law knocked, then appeared in the doorway.

"I hate to ask you this," Mark said, looking at Nancy and me. "But the corpse…" my face must have registered shock, because he hastened to rephrase his sentence, "the person in your room has no identification. I'm wondering if you both could come back and see if you can tell me who it is."

He looked at me apologetically. "I'm sorry to ask you this. I know it will be very upsetting, but before we leave with…her…it would be helpful if we knew who it was. And if there's any next of kin that should be notified."

I stood up and grabbed Nancy's hand. "Come on. We have to do this. And if we're there together, we can hold each other up in case we start to faint."

Claire and Mary Alice started to follow, but Mark stopped them. "It's best if you two remain here," he said.

Well, what could we do but follow him down the hallway to our room? We tried to be quiet, but unfortunately, the door to another room opened and Mary Catherine poked her head out.

"What's going on?" she demanded. "You woke us up.

"And who are you?"

I realized that, since Mark was in plainclothes, there was no way Mary Catherine could have identified him as a member of the Fairport police. And I didn't want to alarm her. I looked at my son-in-law with a question in my eyes.

"I didn't realize there were other guests here tonight," he said. "I'm Detective Mark Anderson of the Fairport police department. There's been an accident, and we were called to investigate."

Mary Catherine looked shocked. As shocked as I was feeling.

Mark gently turned her around and guided her back to her room. "I'll send my partner, Detective Wheeler, to talk to you in a few minutes. In the meantime, please stay in your room."

I was sure that Mary Catherine was dying of curiosity (sorry about that), but obedient Catholic girl that she was, she did as she was told.

I wondered where the other two Marys were. Maybe all three of them had decided to share a room and have their own pajama party. If they did, I hoped they had more fun than we did.

The door to our room was slightly ajar, revealing the police photographer just finishing up his work. And there were two other police officers in the room as well.

I took a deep breath and grabbed Nancy's hand tighter. "Let's get this over with."

We walked into the room and over to the bed. I leaned down and took a good look at the woman.

Oh, rats. Even without my bifocals, I knew who she was.

It was Meg.

Chapter 26

I'm right no matter how wrong I am. And don't you forget it.

"This gives new meaning to pulling an all-nighter," I said, yawning for emphasis. "The last time I didn't get any sleep was when I was studying for a history exam in college."

"Are you sure it wasn't on your honeymoon?" Nancy asked.

"Very funny," I shot back. "Anyway, I'm afraid to look at my face in the bathroom mirror. I know I look terrible. I bet I have bags under my eyes that are huge enough to pack for a week's vacation in Europe."

"Well, you don't look as bad as poor Meg," Claire pointed out. Which was, of course, an excellent point.

"I don't know how I'm going to make it through today," Mary Beth said. "I'm exhausted. Even though I did manage to get a few hours sleep before… Oh, God, I still can't believe it. Poor Meg."

"I just can't believe she's dead," Mary Catherine said. "I absolutely cannot believe it."

Our pitiful reunion committee sat, huddled under quilts, in Claire and Mary Alice's room, trying to wake up and watching the sun rise over a distant Long Island Sound.

"What are we going to do about our reunion?" Mary Ann asked our fearless leader. "Are we going ahead with it? And are we going to tell the rest of the class what happened to poor Meg?"

"We don't really know what happened to Meg," Nancy pointed out. "I mean, Meg died. And Carol and I found her in our room. In one of our beds." She shuddered at the memory. "But we don't know how she died. Or why she was in our room."

"That's right," I said. "Meg wasn't on the guest list. We didn't know she was coming to the reunion. That's really odd. What was she doing here?"

"Maybe she changed her mind and wanted to surprise us," Mary Beth suggested.

"Well, she certainly did that," Claire said. "Poor Meg."

"I think we should just keep this whole thing quiet and go on with the reunion," Nancy said. "I hope that doesn't sound too callous, but we really have no choice. There's no way to contact everybody and tell them not to come."

I nodded my head in agreement.

"But what if the police come back during the reunion to ask more questions?" Mary Beth asked. "How will we explain that?"

"Random bed check?" Claire suggested.

That did it. Either due to total lack of sleep or the need to diffuse our stress, we all started to howl. Giggle. Laugh our stupid heads off.

Yes, it was in very bad taste. I hope you won't tell anybody else about this.

When we'd finally managed to get ourselves under control again, I said, "Ok, everybody, time to hit the showers. I'm sure that'll make us more alert. And I bet the coffee is already on in the dining room. Let's get cracking. We've got a reunion to run."

"Hang on a second," Mary Ann said, motioning all of us to sit down again. "I know we've been saying 'poor Meg,' because she's dead. But when she came back to Fairport a few months ago, she really was 'poor Meg.' At least, that's what she told me. Did she tell any of you that she was broke?"

Mary Catherine looked embarrassed. "I wasn't going to say anything, but since you brought it up, Mary Ann, she hit me up for a loan when she came back to town. She said she'd be able to pay me back very soon. I didn't give her money, but my husband and I let her stay with us for a few nights."

"I thought I was the only one Meg approached for money when she came back to town," Mary Beth said. "I guess not."

"But what happened to her inheritance?" I asked. "I thought her parents left her well-fixed when they died. She used to brag about how wealthy they were, and the big mansion they lived in on Shore Road. Not that I ever got invited there, of course."

"That's what Meg wanted everybody in our class to believe," Mary Ann said. "But her mother worked as the housekeeper in that house on Shore Road, and her father took care of the grounds."

"We were sworn to secrecy," Mary Beth said. "And because we all wore the same school uniforms, it was easy for her to pull that deception off."

"But the tuition," Claire objected. "How did her parents afford it? Mount Saint Francis wasn't cheap."

"Meg was on a scholarship," Mary Catherine said. "She didn't pay for a darn thing."

Chapter 27

My husband gave me an ultimatum: It's either him or the dog. Lord, I'm going to miss that man.

"So, how was the reunion, Mom?" Jenny asked. "I bet you had a blast, judging from how tired you look. Were you up all night partying?"

"Not exactly," I said, taking a forkful of the delicious pot roast Jenny had prepared for our Sunday night supper and chewing it slowly, stalling for time.

"This is so good. And I really appreciate your inviting us to dinner tonight. I didn't get home until after four this afternoon. If I had to start cooking a meal then, we wouldn't have eaten for hours. You know how your father hates to wait. For anything."

I stole a quick look at Jim to see if he'd respond and veer the conversation in another direction. But he didn't rise to the bait. He was too busy eating.

Jenny laughed. "The pot roast should be good, Mom. I used your recipe." She gave her new husband a loving look across the dinner table. "Mark loves it, too."

"But not as much as I love you," Mark responded. Then, he blushed. Just like he used to do when he was a kid.

Fortunately, he'd left his detective persona at the Fairport Police Station.

"I love how you've decorated the condo, Jenny," I said, casting around for other topics of conversation than my reunion. "Is that lamp new?"

"Mom," Jenny said, "for Pete's sake. You and I went shopping for that lamp together. You picked it out. I can tell that you're stalling. Why don't you want to tell us about the reunion? Did you find out some deep dark secrets about some of your classmates that you don't want to share with us?"

"I went to the reunion, too," Jim said, taking a break from his pot roast feeding frenzy. Jenny raised her eyebrows. "I thought guys weren't allowed," she said.

"Well, I didn't go to the actual reunion," Jim said. "I walked through the welcome cocktail party at Maria's Trattoria last night. But I didn't stay too long. I ended up going to the movies with Larry McGee."

"He dropped me off at the restaurant," I explained to Jenny and Mark. "And he had my permission to do a quick walk-through the party. Emphasis on the word 'quick.' He was looking for an old girlfriend."

Oops. Shouldn't have said that.

Jim waggled his eyebrows. "Not just *my* old girlfriend, Carol. She was pretty popular with a lot of the guys in high school. Meg Mahoney." He sighed. "But she wasn't there." He turned to me. "Did she ever show up?"

I looked at Mark for some guidance. And got a tiny head shake. Which I interpreted to mean, "We're investigating. Say as little as possible."

So, ignoring my husband, something I've had years of practice doing, I said brightly, "The reunion lunch was huge success. But it was a good thing we had nametags. So many of the class had changed over the years. Not everyone ages in the same way. I guess it's all in the genes."

Continuing to blather, I said, "The food was terrific. It was a buffet. The catering staff at the facility did an outstanding job. And we had the Seven Deadly Sins for dessert. Do you remember that? We had it on Nantucket at the Grey Gull Inn last year and we all loved it. It seemed to be an appropriate choice for a Catholic girls' high school reunion. Everyone thought it was a riot that we got to choose which sins we wanted in our dessert. Even Sister Rose laughed."

This was good for me, concentrating on the many fun things about the reunion instead of the single horrific one. The more I talked, the more enthused I got.

"Nancy's idea of naming it our Ruby Reunion, rather than our fortieth, was a great idea. All the tablecloths were ruby red, with white napkins. The centerpieces were red and white roses. They were breathtaking. Sister Rose was very pleased. She even joked that we'd chosen roses in her honor."

I laughed.

"We didn't, of course. In fact, that thought never occurred to any of us.

"And we played some funny games, too. One of them was called Name That Nun. It was a take-off on that old television show, *Name That Tune.* You may not remember it. In the reunion program, we had a list of all the nuns who'd taught at Mount Saint Francis while we were there. And we also had a list of all the classes that were offered. The idea was to name which nun taught which class. And there was a prize for the person who got the most correct answers."

I smiled at the memory. "I have to admit that, even though I resisted being involved in the reunion at first, I did have a good time."

I took a sip of water, then continued with my mindless chatter. "Everyone seemed to enjoy the building tours, too. And we even played a game that Sister Rose claimed the nuns used to play in the convent, Sister Says. You know, like the children's game, Simon Says. There was a bit of a mutiny among the class about that, but it didn't last long. And we did laugh a lot."

"I'm glad you had fun, honey," Jim said. "But you still haven't answered my question. Did Meg ever show up?"

I snuck a quick glance at my son-in-law, sitting directly across from me. He refused to make eye contact. The little stinker.

"Well, I think it's safe to say that she did show up, Jim," I said.

Jim beamed. "I knew she would, Carol. Meg always liked to have a good time. How does she look? Has she changed much?"

Hmm. What an interesting question.

"Well, you remember that Meg was briefly on the reunion planning committee, Jim," I said. "So it's not like I haven't seen her recently."

"I know, Carol. You told me. But I noticed that any reunion meetings you hosted here were at times when you knew I wouldn't be home. So I never got the chance to see Meg. And, to my credit, I never asked you about her. Until now.

"So, how does she look? Has she changed much after all these years?"

Help me, I telegraphed to Mark, who immediately jumped up and started clearing away the dirty dishes.

I was on my own.

"I think it's safe to say that Meg didn't look so good when I saw her at the reunion," I said. "Wouldn't you agree, Mark?" I called to my son-in-law, who was headed toward the kitchen with some dishes.

"Mark?" asked Jim. "Why would he have seen Meg?"

There was no way to do this gently, so I blurted it out. "Mark saw Meg last night after I called the police to report finding her dead body in my bedroom."

Chapter 28

I never gossip. I share important information on a need-to-tell basis.

"I guess I have to forgive you," I said to Mark when I finally caught up with him a few days after the reunion. "You're family now. But why did you leave me to do all the explaining to Jim and Jenny about Meg's death? You were there, too, remember? In an official capacity. Nancy and I were just the unlucky people who found her in our bedroom at school. And we didn't even know it was Meg at first. Until you made us come back into the room and identify the ... deceased person."

I fixed my son-in-law with a hard stare, which had no effect on his demeanor whatsoever. The fact that I was sitting in his office at the Fairport Police Station – on his own turf, so to speak – probably had a lot to do with that. If he'd been in my kitchen, I would've had the upper hand.

I was surprised that the local press had ignored Meg's death. After all, a dead body at a high school reunion doesn't happen very often. There wasn't even a brief obituary. I wondered if any next of kin had come forward to take charge of the final arrangements.

And I wondered if I had to attend the funeral. Or how I could get out of it.

I know, I know. I'm a terrible person.

Mark was wearing his official Fairport police detective face today. All business. There was no sign of the nice young kid who used to sit at my kitchen table and do his homework with Jenny all those years ago.

"I didn't mean to put you on the spot," Mark said. Which was probably as close to an apology as I was going to get out of him. "But Meg did die at your reunion. And you and Nancy did find her. I knew you could handle Jim's questions without compromising our official investigation."

"I suppose I should take that as a compliment," I said. But I wasn't letting him off the hook that easily. "What's happened this week? Have you determined the cause of Meg's death? And don't tell me it's none of my business, Mark. As you just pointed out, she was my classmate, and I found her."

Mark leaned back in his chair and thought for a moment. "I guess there's no harm in telling you that we have no reason to suspect that foul play was involved in your classmate's death." He paused. "I shouldn't share this with you."

I sat back in my chair and waited, a technique I've picked up from all the mysteries I read. It wasn't easy. Because, of course, when my son-in-law said he knew something that he shouldn't tell me, I absolutely had to know what it was.

The silence was killing me. (Sorry about that, but it was true.) I finally said, "I won't tell anyone, Mark. I promise. If I'm going to be related to a police detective, I have to learn to keep my mouth shut. I know most of the information you get is confidential. I respect that."

Of course, my fingers were crossed in my lap, but I was hoping that Mark didn't notice.

Mark nodded. "Ok, Carol. It's probably going to come out anyway. Your classmate committed suicide."

I was shocked. "No way, Mark. Meg would never do that."

"She did, Carol. We found a note near her body. Short and to the point. And the toxicology report confirmed it.

"She died from an overdose of Vicodin."

"A drug overdose? Are you sure? I can't believe it. Maybe it was just an unfortunate accident. I can't believe someone I went to high school with would do that."

I shook my head. "No, Mark. You're wrong. Meg did not commit suicide."

"Carol, I understand your reaction. But it's true. The case, if there ever was a case, is closed."

Mark rose to his feet and pointedly looked at his watch, indicating that, as far as he was concerned, our little chat was over.

I sat up straight in my chair and crossed my ankles. Daintily, just like the nuns taught us. "I'm not leaving yet, Mark. In fact, unless you tell me everything you know, you'll have to remove me bodily from your office."

I didn't really mean that, and I prayed he wouldn't take me up on it. Besides, he probably couldn't lift me.

"No way, Carol. I've said too much already. You're really putting me on the spot. I can't tell you anything else until I have clearance to do it from my commanding officer. You don't want me to lose my job, do you?"

"What did the note say, Mark? Can you at least tell me that?"

"Boy, you don't give up, do you?" Mark said, sitting down at his desk again. Was it my imagination that he meant that as a positive thing? Maybe, even admiring my powers of interrogation?

"We could use you in the department. You'd be great wearing down suspects. Anyone would talk to stop you from hammering away at them."

I gave Mark a sweet smile, then got right back to business.

"Now, what did Meg's supposed suicide note say?"

"It said, 'Forgive me,' " Mark said. "Obviously, she wanted forgiveness for what she was about to do. End her life."

"That is just plain ridiculous," I exploded. "Meg never asked anyone for forgiveness in her whole life. She lived her life exactly the way she pleased, and never apologized for anything she did. Because she never thought she had to."

I sat back and considered the so-called suicide note. Then I had a sudden inspiration. "Was there a pill bottle found, too?" I asked.

"Yes," Mark said. "Right next to her body. And it was empty."

Rats. I had been so sure that the police had gotten this all wrong. But it looked like I was the one who had.

I knew when I was licked. “When will Meg’s body be released?” I asked. “And when will the funeral be?”

“A cousin claimed her remains this morning,” Mark said. “Her service will be somewhere in upstate New York. I have no details.”

He slapped his hand on the desk. “And that’s it, Carol. Thanks for coming in.”

Well, don’t let anyone tell you that I can’t take a hint. So I gave my son-in-law a quick peck on the cheek and got the heck out of there.

To go home and ponder the meaning of life. And death. And how it often makes no sense at all.

“Maybe talking to you two about Meg’s death will help me,” I said to Lucy and Ethel. “It’s a good thing that I can make the drive from the Fairport Police Station to our house on autopilot, because that’s what I did today.”

Lucy gave me what I call her reproachful stare. “I know. I should be more careful when I’m behind the wheel. But wait till I tell you what I found out. Maybe then, you’ll understand why I wasn’t concentrating on my driving.”

Ethel padded across the kitchen tiles and stood by the dog biscuit tin. Just in case I didn’t get the message, she made a half-hearted attempt to jump on the counter.

“Ok, I get it. Snacks first, then talking. I guess that’s fair. Psychiatrists charge a lot of money for a consult. You two can be bought for just a few Milk Bones. And I don’t have to make an appointment, either.

“Here, catch.” I tossed each of the dogs a few biscuits, being careful that Ethel got her share as Lucy tend to eat Ethel’s share as well as her own.

"I think we should sit down on the family room couch for an official consultation," I said. "That's what all the pros do."

Grabbing a few more Milk Bones in case their attention waned, the three of us – me in the middle – headed for the next room to snuggle on the couch. Then I got down to business. And told them both the whole, sad story about Meg's death.

They both listened attentively, which is one of the things I love best about dogs. They never complain if I go on and on with a story, urging me to get to the point already – like some humans I could name.

I began to wrap up my story. "So you see, Meg would never commit suicide. That can't be what happened. Even if a pill bottle was found with her…body."

My eyes welled up with tears, which I brushed away angrily. There was no way I'd allow myself to cry for a person who had made my life such a misery in high school.

"And, according to your brother-in-law Mark," Lucy's stubby tail wagged at the mention of his name (he always has treats for the girls when he comes over), "some cousin has already claimed her remains, and she'll be buried in upstate New York. None of us will even have the chance to say goodbye. I think that really stinks."

"And what exactly do you propose to do about that, Carol?" asked My Beloved's voice from the doorway. I jumped a foot. Well, maybe only a couple of inches.

"Jim, you startled me. How long have you been standing there?"

"Long enough to get the gist of what you were telling the dogs," Jim said. "To tell you the truth, even though I usually think your ideas are crazy, you could be right about this."

I wasn't sure at first what I was right about – not being able to attend a memorial service for Meg, or the way she died. But since Jim rarely agrees with me when I allow myself to jump to conclusions, I decided to hear the guy out without interruption. For once.

"I'm not saying that Meg didn't commit suicide," Jim clarified, a thoughtful look on his face. "It's the method that mystifies me. I doubt that she was able to swallow enough pills to cause herself any serious harm, much less kill her."

"And exactly how do you know that, Jim?" I asked. "You hadn't seen her in years. Or, had you?"

"I hadn't seen her since high school," Jim said. "But I remember something that happened while we were on one of our very few dates. It was junior year, and we had gone to the movies. When we came out of the theater, Meg complained of a blinding headache. The kind that makes you sick to your stomach. Do you know what I mean?"

I nodded. I'd never had one that bad, but I knew it could be debilitating.

"I offered to get her some aspirin, but she refused. She told me she couldn't swallow pills. No matter how much water she drank, or how small the pill was, just trying to swallow one made her choke."

"I've heard that some people have problems like that," I said. "I never knew Meg did, though. Of course, why would I? We weren't exactly the best of friends in high school."

"It could be a condition that people outgrow when they reach adulthood," Jim said.

"Of course, you're right," I said. But Jim's story had unsettled me.

"As far as a memorial service for Meg," Jim continued, "I'm sure her family had some sort of service for her in upstate New York. If they chose to make the burial private, that's entirely their prerogative.

"Let it go, Carol. Meg's gone. And there's nothing you can, or should, do about it. Agreed?"

I sighed. For once, I had to agree with him. And I let it go.

Well, of course my resolution to let Meg's death go lasted about as long as it took me to prepare supper, clean the kitchen, and watch an hour of mindless drivel on television. I bet that, if you know me well, you're surprised it lasted that long.

Anyway, at 10:00, right after checking The Weather Channel for the latest forecast, Jim heaved himself out of his chair and announced he was going to bed.

I waited another half hour, until I heard the sound of Jim's snoring, then whispered to Lucy and Ethel, "Come on, girls. We're going to check out a few things on the Internet. But be quiet. Don't wake Jim."

Both dogs raised their heads, sighed deeply, then went back to sleep again.

Ok, I was on my own. I was curious to find out about this difficulty to swallow pills thing that Jim had talked about. And once I got that information, I promised myself that I'd go to bed.

Before I started any research, though, I felt compelled to check my e-mail. I hadn't been online for a few days, which is a record for me. I'm the type who reads her e-mail several times a day. I'm always expecting something of major importance to be there – optimist that I am – and usually get more than my share of spam mail instead.

This time was no different: Important Messages, zip/ Spam Messages, 50. But I realized as I pressed Delete over and over again that I was getting more than my usual alerts from e-book sites. I've always been hesitant to click on one of those links, but what the heck. I was curious.

I was immediately led to a promo for the Book of the Year – that's what the e-book site called it. Yep, you guessed it. *Fifty Shades of Navy.* With everything else that had been going on the last few days, the book had slipped to the back of my radar screen. Where I intended to keep it. Delete. Delete. Delete!

And onward to Google.

Hmm, this was interesting. The Google gurus told me that the inability to swallow pills was a condition called Phagophobia. Emphasis on the word phobia. According to several random Internet sites, Phagophobia is not a physical condition at all. It's a psychological one.

I pondered my new-found knowledge. If Meg had Phagophobia when she was in high school, she could have outgrown it when she got older. Maybe she had an "aha!" moment and decided to get over a childhood phobia. Mind over matter, if you will. For all I knew, she spent some time in therapy to deal with it. And a few other things.

For all I knew.

But the truth was, I didn't know much of anything about Meg the Adult. Except for the fact that, when she showed up in Fairport several months ago after a forty-year hiatus, she was still a pain in the patootie. At least, in my patootie.

What had she done with her life? And – here comes one of the big questions – why the heck did I care? It was more than my usual curiosity, which some people have unfairly labeled my penchant for snooping.

No, if I was going to be completely honest with myself – and if I can't be honest with me, who can I be honest with? – this was personal. Meg's life had ended in what was supposed to be my bed. Or Nancy's bed. Either way, we were involved.

And Meg had left a note. *Forgive me.* Who was that note intended for? And what did she want forgiven? I somehow doubted that it had anything to do with her making fun of my homemade powder blue dress at a freshman year dance.

No matter how I looked at it, Meg was asking for help.

And, by golly, she was going to get it.

Chapter 29

I want to be the wife of the party.

Knowing that Jim's reaction to my conclusions about Meg's death would be of the "What are you, nuts, Carol?" variety, I steered the next morning's breakfast conversation into safer topics. You know the kind I mean, right? What's on your schedule for today, dear? What time do you think you'll be home? Will you pick up something for lunch, or do you want to bring a sandwich with you? And so on. And on.

What I really wanted to know from Jim was when the heck he was getting out of the house, so I could get on the phone and rally the troops – Nancy, Claire and Mary Alice. Of course, because I couldn't wait for him to leave the house, he diddled and daddled in the office for what seemed like an eternity.

So I diddled and daddled myself, taking a leisurely shower, changing the sheets on our bed, anything I could think of in the housekeeping department to pass the time. I refused to get out the vacuum, however. Let him fight the battle of the dust bunnies. He enjoys it much more than I do. My hero.

I finally heard him yell, "Bye, Carol. See you later this afternoon," followed by the slam of the kitchen door, and then – oh, joy – the sound of his car engine revving up.

In no time flat I was on the phone to Nancy, telling her that the police determined Meg had committed suicide, and sharing my own conclusions about Meg's death. "We have to figure this out, Nancy. You know as well as I do that Meg was too self-centered to kill herself. Especially if she had the chance to be the center of attention by showing up at the reunion as a surprise. She wouldn't have missed that for the world. What time today can we get together and brainstorm?"

"I think you're nuts, Carol," my ex best friend said. "But creative. Your thought process always impresses me."

I was tempted to bang the phone down in her ear. But I restrained myself. Instead, I didn't say anything. Not one word.

Sometimes, my self-control amazes me.

Nancy finally got the message. I was angry. And, yes, hurt.

"You know I love you, sweetie," she said. "I'm sorry if I hurt your feelings. But some of us have to earn a living. Mary Alice is working at the hospital today, and I have three open houses to run. Claire and Larry have skipped off for a long weekend in the Berkshires. I guess they wanted to leaf peep before all the leaves were gone. They're staying at the Red Lion Inn. I can give you her cell number."

"I already have Claire's cell number," I snapped back. "I don't need you to give it to me." Yes, I was being snippy. And, yes, I was hurt that I hadn't been privy to Claire and Larry's travel plans, and Nancy had. But hey, I'm a magnanimous person. Not the least bit petty. Despite what you may have been led to believe.

"I'm not going to bother them. Maybe they need some time alone. I hope your open house events go well, and you sell all the properties for above asking price. I'll talk to you soon." And I hung up. Gently.

Of course, I spent the next half hour or so wallowing in self-pity. My usual support network was unavailable. Gone. Vamoosed. On to other things.

I thought about calling Deanna at the hair salon, to see if she could fit me in for a quick styling, but I'd just had my hair done so I'd look extra fabulous for the reunion. And, as Jim is constantly reminding me, we need to watch our pennies. Another visit to Crimpers was not in the cards. Or in the Andrews budget.

So here I was, all alone except for the dogs, carrying a tremendous burden of guilt. Because I knew – I just knew! – that Meg's note was meant for me.

Forgive me, she'd written. *And avenge me.*

Meg really didn't write that last part, of course. But I knew that's what she meant. And I finally figured out who the perfect person was for me to talk to. Someone who was guaranteed to help me put all this in perspective.

Sister Rose.

"Carol, what a nice surprise," said my former high school teacher. "We're very short-handed today. I hope you can pitch in. I could really use you." She propelled me into the back of the shop before I could tell her the reason I'd stopped in, and handed me a purple volunteer apron.

"I'm happy to help for a little while," I said, tying the apron strings around my middle. "But I really came to talk to you. About Meg. And her death."

"Truly tragic," Sister Rose said. "But you girls were right not to make an announcement at the reunion. It would have been…unseemly." She crossed herself. "God rest her soul. I still can't believe she's gone."

"Sister Rose, do you know that the police are ruling Meg's death a suicide?"

"A suicide? One of my girls? Why, that's not possible." Sister Rose looked as shocked and upset as I felt.

"That's just not possible," she repeated. Visibly shaken, Sister Rose turned her back to me. I was unsure if I should continue the conversation or take myself out to the shop itself and tidy up or something. So I just stood there. Like a dope.

"Carol, I need some time alone to adjust to this information. It's very upsetting to me," Sister Rose said.

She turned around to face me. "I'd appreciate it very much if you'd go through the shop and be sure all the merchandise is in order. Unfortunately, customers aren't always considerate about putting clothing they don't want back in the proper places. And would you check the dressing rooms, too?"

"Sure, Sister. I'd be glad to."

Truth to tell (and you better not tell anyone else I admitted this), I was glad of the opportunity to go through the shop on official business for Sister Rose. I confess, I am a retail therapy junkie. Since I was definitely in the dumper because of Meg's death, I figured that cheering myself up by scoring a major bargain in a thrift shop that benefitted domestic violence victims was almost heroic. Saint-like, even.

Even Jim couldn't complain if I made a donation to such a worthy cause, right? Of course, right.

In fact, this was the most cheerful I'd felt since Nancy and I opened the door to our room and found an unexpected, unwelcome guest.

I was whipping through the racks, straightening hangers, arranging clothes in their proper sizes, when the bell above the front door announced the arrival of a customer. Putting on my most friendly smile, I greeted her with a cheery, "Welcome to Sally's Closet. We have the best bargains in Fairport, and all the proceeds benefit such a worthy cause."

"Is Sister Rose here?" the woman asked. She took a closer look at me, then said, "I know you. You're Carol Andrews, right? We met at Mount Saint Francis Academy. Or, I should say, Fairport Manor."

I was embarrassed. "You look so familiar," I said, "but I'm sorry, I can't remember your name. Were you at our reunion?"

The woman laughed. "I was there, but in a staff capacity. I'm J.T. Murray. We met a few months ago when you and some friends came to take a tour of the facility. I'm the marketing director at Fairport Manor."

I realized that a golden opportunity to ask some questions had just fallen into my lap. But I couldn't appear too eager. Or too nosy.

At least, not at first.

It was entirely possible that J.T. had been overseeing last-minute details before the next day's lunch. Maybe she'd even seen Meg arrive.

When in doubt, start with compliments. Then throw in a few casual questions. This technique works most of the time, even on Jim.

"Everything last Sunday ran like clockwork," I said. "We really appreciate all the hard work you must have put in to make the reunion such a success."

I paused, then asked, "Were you at Mount Saint Francis the night before our reunion, too?"

My question seemed to throw J.T. completely off. Her eyes flicked to the right for a millisecond, transmitting that she was about to tell me a whopper of a lie.

"I was there until late Saturday afternoon," J.T. said. "But when the catering staff seemed to have everything under control for the reunion lunch on Sunday, I went home and took a nice, long bath. And went to bed early."

Alone?

I didn't really ask her that, of course. But I wanted to.

"I didn't mean to put you on the spot," I lied right back, "but I'm sure you know that one of our classmates was found dead the night before the reunion. In the room that had been assigned to Nancy Green and me. In fact, Nancy and I are the people who found her.

"The police have ruled Meg's death a suicide, and a cousin has already claimed her remains. She'll be buried in a private ceremony in upstate New York."

"I did hear that someone died the night before your reunion," J.T. said. "That's very sad. I appreciate your bringing me up to date on what the police have concluded."

In a rapid change of subject I found impressive, J.T. continued, "Is Sister Rose here?" She held up a folder. "I have papers that need her signature, and I can't be out of the office too long. We have our very first residents moving in today. It's pretty exciting."

"She's in the back," I said. "Just go through the double doors. And I better get back to work organizing these racks."

But my adventure in retail therapy had lost its appeal, replaced by another one of my favorite pastimes, jumping to conclusions. Because J.T.'s visit had raised many questions in my overworked brain.

Clearly, J.T. didn't tell me the whole truth about her presence at Mount Saint Francis on Saturday. She was even worse at lying than I was. I wondered how late she'd really been at school. Was she the one who greeted Meg and showed her to a bedroom?

Our bedroom? And, if so, why our bedroom, when there were so many others to choose from?

Had she been privy to Meg's arrival plans?

My mind was whirling with possibilities. Or maybe someone from the catering staff had let Meg into the building. They could have been working overtime, prepping for the reunion lunch.

Otherwise, Meg would need an access code to get in the building, the way Nancy and I did.

Then, I realized how stupid I was. The few of us who had made reservations to stay overnight at Mount Saint Francis on Saturday night had been given the access code as part of our Mount Saint Francis Academy Ruby Reunion packet. Meg could have been given the welcome packet and the building access code without involving any staff member.

If that's what had happened, then someone on our committee knew Meg was coming.

Who? And why keep it such a secret?

Unless that same committee person never intended that Meg actually attend the reunion. And took steps to see that she didn't.

Chapter 30

Ever stop to think, and forget to start again?

There was no way I could share my suspicion – ok, another of my wild ideas – with anyone else without thinking it through very carefully. And I knew I couldn't leave the thrift shop until someone else came in to relieve me. As the Good Sister had said, she was short-handed today.

Unless I made up an excuse to leave. And promised to come back later in the week to help out again.

Nah. I dismissed that thought as soon as it flashed through my head. This was Sister Rose I was dealing with. She always saw through my ploys when I was in high school. There was no reason to think her skills in that department had dulled over the years.

When another volunteer backed out of the sorting room holding an armful of clothing, I was tempted to kiss the floor in thanksgiving. Until I realized two things. If I got down on my knees to kiss the floor, I probably wouldn't be able to get up without help. And more importantly, the volunteer who was relieving me at the shop was Mary Catherine – one of my classmates, a fellow reunion committee member, and now on my newly created list of suspects.

Fearful that Mary Catherine was anticipating a cozy chat about the reunion and Meg's death, and unsure about what I should say, I nipped that possibility right in the bud by giving her a quick hug and whispering, "Gotta go. I have a doctor's appointment and I'm going to be late. We'll talk another time."

Then I whipped that purple volunteer apron off and hustled my body out of the thrift shop as fast as I could, mumbling the same lame excuse about my hasty departure to Sister Rose. Fortunately, she was deep in conversation with J.T. and barely heard me.

And I wondered all the way home if it was my imagination that Mary Catherine looked like she wasn't all that thrilled to see me.

In fact, I'd swear she was just as anxious for me to vamoose as I was.

My two canine therapists, Lucy and Ethel, immediately caught on to the fact that I was preoccupied. And they were not pleased with having to share their human's attention with anything or anyone else. When they bounded into the kitchen after taking care of doggie needs in the yard, I just sat at the kitchen table, staring into space, instead of snapping to it and rewarding them with two biscuits, per usual.

Ethel – yes, Ethel! – let out a whine that was so loud it brought me back into focus immediately.

"Yes, ma'am," I said, saluting the pair. "Sorry about the slow service. I've got a lot on my mind."

Things that even a satisfactory snack couldn't ease. Even a chocolate one. (For me, not the dogs.)

So, I gave myself a good talking-to. If I do this in front of the dogs, I can count on them not to squeal on me. Doggie confidentiality and all that stuff.

"Carol, you are really losing it this time. There is no way that any of your classmates could be involved in Meg's death."

I sat back in the chair, satisfied that I had successfully derailed my ridiculous thought process once and for all.

"Oh, yeah?" I argued back. "Have you forgotten about the fact that no one, including Meg's so-called friends, was thrilled when she showed up back in Fairport after all these years and insinuated herself onto the reunion committee? What about that?"

Gosh, I hate it when I argue with myself. I never know which side I'm on.

"This calls for some drastic action," I announced. "I'm going to do something you haven't seen me do for a long time. It'll relieve my stress, and make me feel good. And if I do it right, it won't take too long, either. Although," I frowned, "Jim usually takes care of this for me. He's really good at it, too."

And I went to the hall closet and got out the vacuum cleaner.

Surprised? Why? What did you think I was talking about?

Careful. Remember, I went to Catholic school.

It always amazes me, on the rare occasions that I perform a household task like vacuuming, how doing something completely mindless can make me feel good about myself. For some reason, vacuuming, washing the kitchen floor, or cleaning out a closet clears the cobwebs from my mind as well as the dust bunnies from my floors.

Maybe I should do it more often.

Nah.

Anyway, by the time I was through with the first floor of the house, I had come up with a plan. It was simple, like me. All the mysteries I've read over the years stress the fact that the clues to solve a crime frequently lie within the life of the victim. So, I was going to find out all I could about Meg's life before she came back to Fairport.

And I was going to check out the three Marys, while I was at it.

I switched off the vacuum and plopped myself in a chair in the least-used room in our house – the formal living room – to figure out exactly how I was going to implement my simple, but brilliant, plan. And I realized I needed a partner. A cyber partner.

I would do the in-person interrogations, of course. Remember, even my son-in-law the Fairport detective had complimented me on my interview skills.

But I often get bored, even frustrated, with Internet research. Sometimes I strike gold right away, and find out exactly what I'm looking for. But when I'm searching for something and thousands of possible hits come up, I get disgusted after wading through the first fifty or so and give up.

Fortunately, I came up with the perfect partner – someone I had given birth to more than twenty years ago. My darling son, Mike. Who, although he was a successful restaurant owner in Miami, was usually willing to jump in and help his dear old mother when she needed it. And since his social life was probably in the dumper right now, due to a recent disastrous situation involving a lovely but mysterious young woman from Puerto Rico named Marlee (I think you already know about that), I was betting he had lots of spare time on his hands.

Unless, to heal his broken heart, Mike was throwing himself into the life of a Miami bachelor. And meeting/dating/hooking up with many nubile females who would never pass inspection in the Andrews house. Assuming Jim and I ever met any of them, which was doubtful.

Perhaps this time, when I needed his help so much, my darling son would be too busy between running the restaurant and his active social life to play Internet Doctor Watson to my Shirley – I mean, Sherlock – Holmes.

Then I remembered that Mike was the person who had first alerted me to the YouTube video about that horrible book, *Fifty Shades of Navy*. If I could talk him into checking out Meg Mahoney's past life, maybe he could ferret out the identity of the mysterious author, too.

Mike was already clued in (sorry!) about my high school reunion, too. He just didn't know about the unexpected guest. And her even more unexpected demise. And he, more than Jenny, had inherited the snooping – I mean, sleuthing – gene from me.

The fact that this "assignment" gave me an excuse to check up on him – not that I ever meddle in his life, of course – made my plan even more appealing. Absolutely perfect, in fact. One of my best.

I had successfully deluded myself into thinking that my son would jump at the chance, one more time, to help me out. So I fired off a quick e-mail giving the bare bones of "Guess Who Came To The Reunion And

Didn't Leave Alive?" And forced myself to give Mike the rest of the day to respond.

I never push my children. I am the soul of patience while I win them over to my point of view. No matter how long it takes. Honest.

I decided to start the in-person interrogation part of my investigation with Neecy. It was possible that she had no time to talk to me, of course, with the election for state senate less than a month away. I needed to make her an offer she couldn't refuse.

At that moment, Lucy made a flying leap and landed on my lap. "Hey, Lucy," I said, shooing her down, "you know you're not allowed on the living room couch. In fact, you and Ethel aren't supposed to be in here at all."

Lucy gave me a doggy stare, the kind she does when she's trying to tell me something and I'm too stupid to figure out what it is.

Enlightenment dawned. "Brilliant, Lucy," I said, heading toward the telephone. "That's a great idea. I'll call Neecy and suggest a doggie play date for you and Ethel with Neecy's chocolate lab. That way, you two can be a diversion and have fun with Porter, while I'm grilling Neecy about Meg.

"Thanks, Lucy," I said, reaching down and giving her head a loving pat. "I owe you an extra biscuit for that idea."

Lucy telegraphed a look that told me, loud and clear, that I better be quicker on the uptake the next time. Swear to God. And she didn't work that cheap. This brainstorm was worth at least three dog biscuits. And I better include three biscuits for Ethel, too, because they always worked as a team.

The biscuit compensation would be well worth it if Neecy could clear up some information for me. Starting with the identity of the wealthy family that Meg's parents had worked for.

And I vowed to be so subtle that Neecy would never even realize she was being interrogated.

As I was reaching for the phone to invite myself and my canine co-conspirators to Neecy's – I had already decided that I wanted to check out her house, too – I stopped myself.

"You know," I said to the dogs, who by now had devoured down their treats and returned to napping under the desk in my office, "it might work better if I brought another human along on our little adventure. It's not that I think any less of your detective skills, understand. You've both already proved how good you are. But another set of ears could be helpful to me, and after all, you'll both be running around the yard with Porter."

The only response I got from either dog was the sound of snoring. Loud snoring. Hmm. They sounded like Jim.

I ruled out calling Nancy again. She had shot down my idea without even hearing me out. That hurt my feelings. Forget her. And Claire was romping around the Berkshires with her favorite local lawyer.

That left Mary Alice, the only member of my immediate posse who might be available, assuming her nursing stint at the hospital was over. And, more importantly, she might look on this as a change of pace from her non-adventurous life.

I took a chance and called Mary Alice first, leaving a cryptic message about an invitation to an adventure that she'd definitely want to be part of. "Call me as soon as you get this," I ended.

Satisfied that I had conveyed my message with the proper balance of hype and urgency, I called Neecy's cell phone.

She picked up on the second beep, and from the noise emanating from her end of the phone, I had interrupted some sort of party.

"What? Who? Oh, Carol. I'm so glad you called. But you'll have to talk louder. I can't hear you," Neecy said. "Hang on a minute. I have to find a quiet corner."

I heard the sound of a jazz trio in the background, then applause. I figured she must be at a party, and I was embarrassed I'd intruded.

"Neecy, I'll call you tomorrow," I said. "This is obviously not a good time for you to talk."

"It's a perfect time, Carol," Neecy said. "I'm at a fundraising event for Tony's campaign. I'm bored to death, and trying not to show it."

I explained my idea about a play date for our dogs as quickly as I could. "I know this is short notice. and you probably have a full calendar of campaign commitments, Neecy. But I'm not sure how much longer the weather will be warm enough for the dogs to play outside. What do you think?"

Yes, I know that was lame. But it was the best I could come up with on the spur of the moment. I held my breath, hoping that Neecy would say yes.

"It's a perfect time, Carol," Neecy said. "I'll be there in a minute."

"What? I'm confused," I said. "Do you mean you want to meet now?"

"No, Carol." Neecy laughed. "I was telling Tony that I'd be back in a minute to stand by his side as his adoring wife while he made his speech. That's my primary job these days.

"I do have to hang up now, though. And it's my turn to host a doggie play date. So how about if you bring Lucy and Ethel to play with Porter tomorrow around noon? We'll have a salad or something light for lunch and catch up while the dogs amuse themselves outside."

I couldn't believe how well this was working out. And, of course, I was excited to see Neecy's house. I'd heard from other sources that it was drop-dead gorgeous, like something out of a magazine.

"Please don't go to any trouble, Neecy."

"Don't worry about that, Carol. I'm so glad you're coming tomorrow," Neecy said. "I wanted to talk about Meg with someone who knew her. I still can't believe she's gone." She rattled off an address in a gated community north of the Merritt Parkway and was gone.

I couldn't believe my luck. Because I certainly wanted to talk about Meg, too. I could hardly wait until tomorrow.

Chapter 31

I'm not old. I'm chronologically gifted.

"I'm glad you asked me to go with you and the girls today," Mary Alice said. "I've missed taking care of them. You know you can call me any time to come and walk them, even if you're only going to be gone a little while."

"I know I can," I said. "And I appreciate it. The dogs have missed seeing you, too, as I'm sure you can tell from the enthusiastic greeting you got from both of them."

Mary Alice laughed. "It's been quite a while since I was kissed so enthusiastically."

I squelched the response that sprang into my brain before it had a chance to reach my mouth. *What's up with the online dating thing? Had any good dates lately?*

But, of course, when you've been friends for as long as Mary Alice and I have, you can read each other's thoughts.

"I know you're wondering what's happening with my love life these days, Carol. Thanks for not cross-examining me about it. Let's just say that I've met a lot of frogs over the past several months, but so far I haven't found a prince to kiss. Internet dating isn't all it's cracked up to be." She slid me a sideways glance. "But you'll be the first one I tell if I finally meet someone who seems like a prime candidate."

I reached over and patted her hand. "Any guy would be lucky to date you," I said like the loyal friend I am. "And today, I'm saving my cross-examining skills to use on Neecy. Having you along is a real bonus, and should make getting information about Meg easier."

"Assuming Neecy has any information that we don't already know," Mary Alice reminded me. "Didn't she say she hadn't heard from Meg in years?"

I nodded. "That's true. But I'm betting that she can fill in some blanks on Meg's years in Fairport. For instance, who was the wealthy family that Meg's parents worked for?

"I guess we're here," I said, swinging my Jeep into a pebbled driveway that led to a house bigger than mine, Nancy's and Claire's put together.

"Wow. This is some place," I said. "It reminds me of an English country estate."

"I know," Mary Alice said. "The house looks like a smaller version of *Downton Abbey.*" At my questioning look, she clarified. "Don't you ever watch *Masterpiece Classic* on PBS, Carol?"

I shook my head. "Jim and I don't watch much television these days. Except The Weather Channel, of course." I was not about to admit that I am hopeless addicted to *Say Yes To The Dress* on TLC. Or the Home and Garden network. I got hooked on *Say Yes To The Dress* when Jenny was looking for a wedding gown last year. And I've always suffered from house lust.

I suppose you're all thinking that I'm easily impressed. Maybe even criticizing me for being bowled over by what was, by my standards, a mansion. I forgive you. And if you're ever lucky enough to be invited to Neecy's house, I know you'll say that I didn't exaggerate. Just this once.

I parked the Jeep beside the farthest bay of the four-car garage. "This house has more wings than a heavenly choir," I said, smoothing the wrinkles from my chinos and attempting to look presentable. "I never expected anything this grand.

"Let's ring the bell first, before we get Lucy and Ethel out of the back. Just in case we have the wrong house. There was no name on the mailbox at the bottom of the driveway, and I don't want to be embarrassed. In this ritzy neighborhood, if we're at the wrong address, the owners are liable to call the police."

"I wouldn't worry about that," Mary Alice said. "You have a relative by marriage on the force, and he'll vouch for you."

Maybe not all the time. And especially if I'm poking my nose into something I shouldn't be. Like now, for example.

I didn't really admit that to Mary Alice, of course.

Neecy must have been watching for us, because the heavy oak door flew open before I could even ring the bell. She gave me a quick peck on the cheek. "I try to head guests off before they ring the bell," she said. "The sound makes Porter bark like the dickens, and it takes forever to quiet her down.

"Mary Alice!" Neecy said, throwing her arms around my traveling companion. "I'm so glad you came, too. I don't entertain too much these days. In fact, we're usually not home with all these crazy campaign events we have to attend. I'll be happy when it's all over."

"And you'll be even happier when I win the election," said a deep masculine voice from the top of the staircase.

"Well, of course I will be, Tony," Neecy said. "I thought you'd already left for the Kiwanis luncheon. Come and say hello to some friends from high school."

Wow. I mean, WOW. If I was dazzled by the house, I was even more dazzled by Neecy's husband.

My immediate impression was of a man in his late fifties who took very good care of himself. Not too tall. Not too short. An athletic build (no evidence of the extra poundage that My Beloved was carting around), gray hair that caressed his neck (but neatly – not shaggy), clean-shaven (no salt-and-pepper beard that some men attempt to grow in their later years in a vain attempt to hide a flaccid jowl line). Beautiful brown eyes. What we used to call "bedroom eyes." Well-dressed, but not dressed up. Business casual, I think it's called.

But all of this was just the icing on the cake. The man exuded charisma. Lordy, I would have followed him anywhere. And when he took both of my hands in his, I almost melted into a warm puddle right there in the foyer.

"Carol Kerr," Tony said, giving my hands a firm squeeze, "I'd know you anywhere. You were beautiful in high school, but you're even more beautiful now."

I laughed self-consciously, a flush creeping up my neck. It was a long time (like, never) that anyone ever told me that I was beautiful.

"I bet you say that to all Neecy's classmates," I quipped.

Gosh, Carol, what a stupid thing to say. Couldn't you come up with something more intelligent than that?

"And you're Mary Alice Bennett," Tony said, turning his considerable charm onto my usually shy friend and achieving the same effect with her as he had with me.

Neecy linked her arm through Tony's and gave him a wifely peck on the cheek. "He cleans up well," she said. "Usually, if he's going to a construction site, he's in jeans and work boots. But since he's running for state senate, he's spiffed up his wardrobe."

Tony laughed. "Neecy's right. She knows me too well. And she's been very supportive and understanding about my decision to run for office. Even if it takes me away from home more than she'd like."

Recovering myself and trying to act like the grown-up person I'm supposed to be, I said, "I'm surprised that you recognized us after so long, Tony. I don't think I'd have recognized you if I hadn't seen your picture in the paper so often recently."

"Well, it helped that Neecy clued me in that you were coming today," Tony admitted with a grin. "But, believe me, I would have known you anyway, even if she hadn't told me. Sometimes I think that, the older I get, it's easier for me to remember people from my younger days than someone I've just met. Which can be a problem when you're running for office, like I am. I'm supposed to remember the names of everyone I'm introduced to. And at least one pertinent fact about that person, too. That's what fills the campaign coffers and makes people want to volunteer to help me win this election."

A cynical view of the political process, to be sure. But probably an accurate one.

"Oh, I almost forgot, Tony," Neecy said. "You had a phone call while you were in the shower. The college students who were coming into headquarters to get that mailing out won't be able to help after all. The office is trying to find some other volunteers, but so far, have been unsuccessful."

"The timing couldn't be worse," Tony said, clearly upset at Neecy's news. "We need to get those brochures into voters' mailboxes by the weekend. We've spent weeks writing the copy and building a targeted list for this mailing."

And suddenly I heard someone ask, "How many pieces are in the mailing? Maybe I could help."

Good lord, that was me.

Chapter 32

My parents taught me to respect my elders.
But at my age, I have no one to respect.

"He has that effect on everybody, Carol," Neecy said. "But it's a pretty quick recovery, thank goodness."

Mary Alice, Neecy and I were finishing a delicious low-cal lunch on Neecy's expansive porch. The rear wall of windows gave us a perfect way to keep tabs on the three canines, who were running around a large, fenced-in area chasing heaven knows what. And having a great time.

"Tony certainly is a charismatic person," I said.

And sexy as hell. I didn't really say the last part, of course.

Neecy laughed. "You don't really have to do that mailing, Carol. I know how persuasive those big brown eyes can be. I can find someone else to pitch in."

"No, Neecy, I'm happy to do the mailing," I said. Even though I was hypnotized into it. "Jim is so involved in local politics, and he's always talking about people and issues that I know very little about. It's time I got more involved."

"I'll help, too," Mary Alice said. "After all, we're Mount Saint Francis girls. We should help each other out more often. And I have to admit, those brown eyes are pretty persuasive. I wish I'd find somebody like him through my online dating service."

"As I said, he has that effect on everyone," Neecy said. Then she frowned. "Well, everyone except my parents. They said he was a bad influence on me, and did everything they could to break us up."

I nodded. "I remember you told me this at lunch, Neecy. It must have been very difficult. You and Tony were a modern-day Romeo and Juliet."

"I never thought about it that way," Neecy said. "You're right. A forbidden boyfriend who wore a black leather jacket and rode a motorcycle was irresistible to me. And, as you said, there were those brown eyes."

My toes curled at the memory.

Mary Alice looked at me and shook her head a little. She was right. It was time to move the conversation along.

"Now that Meg is gone," I began, "I'm realizing that, even though we went to high school together, I never really knew her at all. For instance, I always thought Meg's family was rich. I found out recently that wasn't true. Meg's mother was the housekeeper for a wealthy local family, and her father took care of the grounds. I wonder who that family was."

"That's an easy one, Carol," Neecy answered. "Meg's parents worked for my family. Although, the way Meg acted most of the time, you'd think that it was the other way around."

I choked on my iced tea, and spilled it all over the tablecloth.

"Oh, Neecy, I'm so sorry," I said, totally embarrassed and trying to blot up my mess with a napkin.

"I'm the one who's sorry," Neecy said as Mary Alice handed me another napkin. "My timing was bad. I didn't mean to make you choke. Let me pour you a fresh glass of iced tea. And don't worry about the tablecloth. It's machine-washable."

Neecy's hands shook as she attempted to pour me a fresh glass. "I guess I'm nervous," she said. "I've never told anyone the real story about Meg and me before. Tony knows, of course, because he's part of it. Excuse me a minute. I'll be right back."

Mary Alice and I sat in silence for a moment. "I don't blame Neecy for being nervous," I finally said. "I think I'm nervous, too. I'm not really sure I want to hear what Neecy has to say."

We heard the sound of water running in the kitchen, then the tap of Neecy's feet as she hurried back onto the porch. She looked much calmer now.

"Sorry about that," Neecy said. "It's wonderful what washing your face can do. Now, where was I?'

"You'd just told us that Meg's parents worked for your family," Mary Alice said. "And," looking at me, "that's when Butterfingers here spilled iced tea all over the tablecloth."

"Thanks for that reminder, Mary Alice," I said. "I'll get even with you later."

Neecy laughed. "It must be wonderful to have a friend you can say something like that to, and not hurt that person's feelings."

"Who says Carol didn't hurt my feelings?" Mary Alice asked, smiling.

"Backatcha, girlfriend," I said, returning her smile with one of my own.

"Everyone at school thought Meg and I were best friends," Neecy said. "Like you two are. But we weren't. Far from it. In fact, to tell the truth, I really hated her."

Join the club.

"Meg worked very hard to make everyone believe she was a rich little Fairport princess. Of course, in order to do that, she needed someone to help her. Me."

Neecy sighed. "I guess I should tell you both the whole story."

I wanted to say, "Spill it." But I didn't.

"Meg's parents came to work for my family when I was fourteen years old. At first, I was thrilled to have someone exactly my age living in our house."

Neecy held up her hand. "Slight correction. Meg wasn't actually living in our house. She and her family lived in a cottage on the grounds. We became good friends. At least, from my point of view. I was very lonely, the typical overprotected poor little rich girl. And, as things turned out, a real jerk, too."

Neecy took a deep breath. "When Meg first came, we were very close," she went on. "I even lent her some of my clothes. And we shared secrets. Lots of secrets." Neecy giggled. "Maybe, too many secrets.

"Anyway, I bet you'll be surprised to hear that Tony – my Tony – dated Meg before he dated me. But he chose me instead of her. How about that?"

It was hard to know where to go with the conversation after an announcement like this. Even for someone as nosy as me.

"Meg was in my room all the time, helping herself to clothes she could wear for some hot date," Neecy said. "My parents thought it was wonderful that I had such a close friend. Hah! I wonder what they would have said if they knew how often she'd saunter into the house, go up to my bedroom, and take something from my closet."

She shook her head. "Never mind. I bet they would have said that I should be flattered that Meg wanted to wear my clothes. They thought she was the best thing ever. At times, I thought they loved her more than me."

"I don't understand, Neecy," I said. "Meg was stealing clothes from you. And you let her get away with it. Why didn't you try and stop her?"

I couldn't help myself. This made no sense to me.

"I wanted to be popular, Carol. For heaven's sake, can't you understand that? I was only popular at school because everyone thought I was Meg's best friend. Hanging out with her was like getting the Good Housekeeping Seal of Approval. I would have done anything to keep that image going.

"Then, one night, Tony came to pick her up for a movie date. Meg and I were outside, and I remember she was twirling around, showing off a brand new dress that my mother had just bought me. Of course, I hadn't worn it yet. Not that she cared about that.

"Tony came roaring up the driveway on his motorcycle. When I saw him, I thought my heart would burst out of my chest. Meg hopped on the back of the motorcycle, but before they roared down the driveway, he turned around and gave me the sweetest, most loving look. And I knew, right then and there, that we were meant to be together. The next day he called me for a date. My parents forbade it, of course. So I snuck out to meet him. It was…thrilling."

Neecy closed her eyes, smiling at the memory. "I can still see him that night. He was so handsome. Well, of course, he still is."

She snapped back to the present. "Tony called me again, and my mother refused to let me talk to him. So he waited for me outside Mount Saint Francis. And he asked me if I wanted to go for a ride on his motorcycle. Oh, man, did I ever! It was so much fun. So…freeing. I loved it."

Neecy frowned. "When my parents found out, they were furious. I always thought that Meg was the one who squealed on me. She denied it, of course. But she was so jealous when Tony dropped her to start taking me out."

A smile curved on her lips. "I think that was the only time in our lives that I had something she wanted, that she couldn't take from me. Meg couldn't figure out why Tony preferred me to her. And, to tell you the truth, neither could I. But I didn't care. I fell for him the first night I laid eyes on him. And he felt the same way about me.

"Nobody but Meg knew we were dating. Believe it or not, she covered for me at home lots of times. Of course, there was a price to pay. Meg always demanded payment, in one form or another, for doing someone a favor. Especially me.

"And soon after graduation, Tony and I eloped."

"It sounds like you and Tony were meant to be together," Mary Alice said.

"That's true. But I'm not going to pretend that we've lived happily ever after," Neecy said. "No one does. We've had a good life. Until our son died. I didn't think either of us would survive that." She pressed her lips together. "I'm not going to cry. I've shed gallons of tears since we lost Anthony."

"The death of a child has to be the most horrible thing that can happen to a parent," I said. "I can't imagine the pain you and Tony went through."

Mary Alice flashed me a warning glance. She sensed that I was about to ask more questions. I got the message and took a sip of my iced tea instead.

"Anthony was just eighteen when he died," Neecy said. "Legally, that meant he was an adult. But he always was my baby boy.

"Unfortunately, he made some bad choices. He died of a drug overdose. I was the one who found him."

Nobody spoke. Mary Alice and I watched helplessly as huge tears gushed out of Neecy's eyes.

I realized that I was crying myself.

"Meg showed up at Anthony's funeral," Neecy said after taking some time to compose herself. "She was his godmother. A very poor choice on our part, in hindsight. But my parents insisted on her, so Tony and I agreed.

"Meg really came to the funeral so she could hit us up for money, not share in our sorrow or comfort us. As usual, it was all about her."

"What a heartless bitch!" I said. Mary Alice shook her head at me. But I couldn't help myself.

"She was what she was, Carol," Neecy said. "I believe your phrase sums her up quite nicely." She allowed herself a ghost of a smile. "I've sometimes wondered if she was glad Anthony died. That his death was my punishment for stealing Tony away from her all those years ago."

"That was the end of your so-called friendship, right?" I asked. "You said you hadn't seen Meg in a long time."

"I didn't tell you the truth about that," Neecy said. "I didn't tell Tony, either. But every now and then she'd contact me and say she needed money. And I always gave it to her."

"But why?" I asked. "She made your life miserable."

"Let's just say that Meg knew some things about me that I preferred to keep hidden," Neecy said.

"I'm not going to tell you that part. We all have our secrets."

I didn't have to look at Mary Alice to know that she was telegraphing me not to probe. And, to my credit, I didn't.

"Of course, each time Meg contacted me," Neecy said, "the amount she asked for increased. And then she showed up at my door a few months before the reunion. She was very excited. She told me that she was onto something that was going to make her a rich woman very soon."

"Did she tell you what it was?" Mary Alice asked.

"No," Neecy said. "Not even a tiny hint. But it was like she'd won the lottery – that's how excited she was.

"And it seems to me that if Meg was about to become rich, it makes no sense that she would commit suicide," Neecy said. "I think someone murdered her. And I'm afraid that if it comes out how much I hated her, and that I've been giving her money for years, the police will think it was me.

"So I want to hire you to find out how Meg died, Carol. I know you've done this kind of thing a few times in the past. I have no one else I can turn to."

She slid a personal check, made out to me, across the table. "Fill in any amount you want."

Chapter 33

Bet you didn't know that the 11th Commandment is "Thou Shalt Not Stick Thy Nose Into Other People's Business." I tend to ignore that one.

It takes a lot to stun me into silence. No surprise, right? But Neecy's offer to pay me was a first. I didn't know how to answer her.

I'd never thought that being a natural snoop could open up a new career path for me. After all, Miss Marple never collected a paycheck, and look at all the mysteries she solved.

I wanted to say, "Of course I can help you, Neecy. I'll figure out how Meg died. And keep you out of it."

But I knew better. Because it was possible, though unlikely, that Neecy was involved in Meg's death. After all, she had just admitted to Mary Alice and me that she'd been giving good old Meg money for years to keep a secret. Any way I looked at that, it was blackmail. Hush money.

On the other hand, if Neecy was involved in Meg's death, she wouldn't have asked me to help her, right? Unless she enlisted me because she figured I could find out information she couldn't. And she could use that information to cover her tracks, so to speak.

Lordy, what a mess. I didn't know what I should do.

So I used one of my most time-honored techniques, honed through years of practice dodging questions from Jim about the cost of my recent retail purchases – I didn't give her a direct answer.

"I can't take money from you, Neecy," I said. "But we all want to know how Meg died," I said. "In fact, we were talking about that very thing on the ride over here today, weren't we, Mary Alice? And you came up with the idea of a tribute or memorial celebration for Meg," I said. "Especially since none of our class was able to attend her funeral.

I hoped Mary Alice would go along with my spur-of-the-moment brainstorm.

"The more I think about your idea, the better I like it, Mary Alice. And it's so fitting that you organize it, since you were our class president."

Now I snuck a peek at Mary Alice, whose face resembled a thundercloud. "I don't remember saying...."

"And I said I'd help you." I continued. "We talked about involving Sister Rose, too."

"I guess we did talk a little about a service," Mary Alice said, now still looking annoyed but finally catching on to what I was up to.

"That's an interesting idea, considering Meg didn't have a whole lot of friends in our class," Neecy said. "I suppose we could do something. We could even hold it here."

Then she veered back to her outrageous job offer. "But we can't do anything until we know more about how she died. And prove that I'm not involved. So it all comes down to you, Carol. Are you going to help me?"

Rats. Now I know how a deer felt when it was trapped in the headlights of an oncoming car.

"I'll see what I can find out," I said. "No promises, though. And absolutely no money."

Neecy jumped up and gave me a big hug. "Thanks, Carol. I knew I could depend on you."

I made a big show of looking at my watch. "It's almost four o'clock, Mary Alice. Don't you have to be at the hospital by five? We'd better collect the dogs and go."

Right now. Before I got myself into any more trouble.

Jim wasn't going to be thrilled to hear about my official sleuthing. And my son-in-law, well, his reaction didn't bear thinking about.

I was heading outside to corral Lucy and Ethel when Neecy followed me to the front door, holding two boxes. “Don’t forget about Tony’s mailing, Carol,” she said. “Unless you won’t have the time to do it now.”

“Not a problem,” I lied, grabbing the boxes and heading toward my car. “Not a problem at all.”

At least, not a problem compared to the mess I currently found myself in. Stuffing envelopes would be a welcome, mindless diversion.

My specialty, since my mind had gone AWOL a long time ago.

Chapter 34

I changed my computer password to "incorrect." That way, if I log in with the wrong one, the computer will tell me, "Your password is incorrect." Brilliant, right?

"Of course, I turned down Neecy's job offer," I said to Jim. "Although I have to admit I was flattered she wanted to hire me. It's the first job offer I've had in a long time."

I had decided to give my husband a carefully edited synopsis of the day's events. Which I had come up with on the way home from Neecy's and practiced first on Mary Alice, and then on Lucy and Ethel. I can always depend on their approval.

Well, I usually can.

"Carol, when I suggested that you add to our retirement income with some sort of part-time employment, opening a detective agency wasn't what I had in mind," Jim said.

"How about my becoming a political campaign consultant?" I asked. "Neecy's husband needed help getting a mailing out and I volunteered. He's the kind of person it's hard to refuse. Very charismatic."

And sexy as all get-out. I didn't really say the last part, of course. No point in giving Jim anything like *that* to worry about.

"I never would have figured Tony Prentiss to be a success at anything when we were growing up," Jim said. "Much less run for elected office. I think that he was arrested once in high school for stealing a car."

"You can't be serious, Jim. Tony's a successful businessman, not a car thief."

"Carol, we all were young once. And did some stupid things. All I know is, Tony ran with a dangerous crowd when we were in high school."

"Well, Tony must have straightened himself out," I said, defending my friend's husband. "He certainly wouldn't be running for office if he had a criminal background. As a matter of fact, by my standards, he's testimony to what the love of a good woman can do. So, there, Mr. Smarty Pants. And I'm glad to help him out by doing this mailing. I hope he wins the election, too."

Jim settled himself into a kitchen chair and grabbed a handful of campaign literature. "I think it's a little late for you to begin a career in politics, Carol. How about if I knock off some of this mailing while you make dinner. I'm starving."

That man really does have a two-track mind.

I couldn't wait for Jim to go to bed that night. I was anxious to check my e-mail and see if my darling son had responded to my urgent message. And I didn't want to answer any more questions from my husband, since after 10:00 p.m., my creative juices totally dry up and I tend to tell Jim things that I'd never admit earlier in the evening.

Finally, having relieved his mind that Fairport, Connecticut, was not in imminent danger of any major weather-related calamities, thanks to the assurance of the all-knowing meteorologists at The Weather Channel, Jim heaved himself out of his chair and announced he was going to bed.

"I want to check my e-mail, dear. I won't be long," I said. Jim nodded and headed to the bedroom.

And I logged onto the computer.

Halleluiah! A message from Mike.

Hey Cosmo girl. What's up with u? R u in trouble again?

I began typing my reply so fast that I misspelled most of the words. Oh well, Mike would get the idea. And maybe he'd even think I'd invented a new language.

I ended with: *Need u 2 do Internet search right away. Do u have time 2 help?*

Then I fired it off and waited. I was proud of myself that I'd inserted a few words in "textese." Hey, I keep up with current trends.

The response came immediately. Just like I'd hoped.

Mike: *Restaurant closed 4 a week. Painters here. Search 4 what?*

I rattled off a bunch of names for him to check out: Meg Mahoney (a.k.a. Mary Margaret Mahoney), Neecy Prentiss (a.k.a. Denise Prentiss and Denise Nolan), and the three Marys. Also Tony Prentiss.

Once again, a reply:

Mike: *What do u want to know about them?*

Me: *Everything. What have they been doing 4 the last 40 years?*

Mike: *Everything? U sure r nosy.*

Me: *Ha! As much info as u can find. Especially about Meg Mahoney. She died at the reunion. Well, right b4 the reunion.*

Mike: *Aha! I knew there was a dead body in there somewhere. Bet you're involved. Was she ur roommate?*

Me: *No, but she was found in my room. By me.*

Mike: *Ouch.*

Me: *Especially 4 her.*

Mike: *Leave it 2 me. But give me a little time.*

Me: *Don't do anything illegal!*

Mike: *I'll take my cue from u.*

Somehow, I didn't find that comforting.

Well, after that cyber conversation with Mike – during which I did not ask about his current (or past) romantic life, which just about killed me – I was wide awake. Like I'd just gulped down 4 cups of high-test coffee. Black.

I knew I'd never get to sleep until I wound down. And I also knew that, if I snuck into bed and tried to go to sleep, my tossing and turning would drive Jim nuts. Not that I could blame him, the poor guy. When I'm this fired up, late at night, even Lucy and Ethel want nothing to do with me.

Unfortunately, Jim and I had already finished Tony's campaign mailing. I considered taking the brochures out of the envelopes so I could re-stuff them. Then I remembered that we had sealed them. Too bad we were so efficient.

The siren song of a sleeping computer lured me back to my desk. "At least you won't mind if I wake you up," I said. "Maybe I have a new e-mail that I need to check out."

Nada. Zip. Boring. But not boring enough to put me to sleep.

I was so desperate for late-night entertainment that I decided to check out my Spam folder. I often found things in there that were so ridiculous, they made me laugh out loud. Like an offer of marriage from an Arab sheik who found himself wrongfully jailed in another country and needed $10,000 from me to spring him, so he could buy me the engagement ring he had promised me.

Hmm. It seemed that I'd gotten several e-mails from Amazon suggesting titles for me to buy. And most of them suggested *Fifty Shades of Navy*.

I'd meant to give Mike this book to research, too. But he already had so many other things to check out.

I'm a pretty obedient person. If someone in authority suggests that I should do something, I usually do it. And who has more authority in this entire cyber universe than the biggest cyber bookstore?

I can talk myself into anything. It's a gift.

So, why not do this myself? All I had to do was click on the Amazon link. Not that I planned to order the book. Of course not. But maybe I could find out a little more about the book, and the author, without committing myself to a sale.

Oh, grow up, Carol. You're a married woman. You don't shock easily.

So, I clicked. And was immediately on the book's Amazon page.

The cover art was a pair of navy knee socks, artfully draped over a pair of…omg…were those handcuffs? Nah. I must be imagining things.

I forced my eyes away from the cover to read the author blurb:

There has been much speculation in the media about the identity of this book's author. For reasons of confidentiality, however, the publisher can only confirm that the writer has direct, personal knowledge of growing up as a Catholic girl in the Sixties and Seventies. It was this intimate knowledge that inspired the story of Fifty Shades of Navy.

Rats. I'd never get to sleep now.

Chapter 35

I don't have a problem with caffeine.
But I have a HUGE problem without it.

"I'm getting way too old to pull all-nighters," I moaned to Lucy while I was looking at my haggard face in the bathroom mirror. Lucy remained unsympathetic. She's used to me moaning and groaning first thing in the morning.

And, as my canine sidekick was pointing out to me with a disgusted stare, I didn't really pull an all-nighter. I did get two hours' sleep.

Which only made me feel worse. Like I'd been hit by a train but didn't have the good sense to die right then and there.

Groan.

"How am I ever going to get through the day? I'm absolutely exhausted."

Put your tasks in priority order and you'll be fine, Lucy advised. *Starting with serving Ethel and me our breakfast.*

Swear to God, that's what she said.

I stumbled into the kitchen and was startled to see Jenny sitting at the table. My mom-o-meter immediately ratcheted up several degrees. Was there trouble in newlywed-land?

Not that I would ever come right out and ask her, of course. Remember, I'm very subtle, and I never interfere in my children's lives.

"You look terrible, Mom," my favorite daughter said. She pushed her coffee mug in my direction. I saw it was the one I gave her for her tenth birthday, the one that proclaimed, "Congratulate me. I'm a double digit, now."

"Sit down and inhale some of this coffee. You look like you need it more than I do."

"Thanks, sweetie," I said, plopping my aging body into a chair. "You're right. I do need coffee. And I know I look terrible. Sleep deprivation has that effect on me."

Jenny wrinkled her brow. "Why didn't you get any sleep?" Then, she grinned. "Did you and Dad have a wild night?"

"We take our cue from you and Mark," I shot back, embarrassed at her insinuation.

Jenny blushed.

Oh, Carol. You went too far with that crack.

"Sorry, sweetie," I said, squeezing her hand. "That was out of line. Your married love life is none of my business."

"I'm the one who should apologize," Jenny said. "My crack was way out of line, too. I didn't mean to embarrass you."

She leaned over and gave me a quick peck.

"So, why are you up and about so early?" I asked. "Do you have a class to teach this morning? Or…" I searched my daughter's face… "is something up with you? Everything ok? With you and Mark, I mean."

Sheesh, Carol. Stifle yourself, already.

"Of course everything's all right," Jenny said. "More than all right. Blissful. No need for you to worry.

"But last night Mark and I talked a little more about what happened at your reunion. It must have been awful, finding someone dead in the bed you were supposed to sleep in. Ugh." She grimaced. "You've had far too many of those adventures lately."

"It was horrible," I admitted. "And, you're right. This has been happening to me too often. Sometimes, I wonder if I'm cursed. Is this the way my golden years are going to play out – going from one crime to another? AARP never did a workshop on this."

"You need to protect yourself, Mom. Don't get involved. You're not as young as you used to be."

"Thank you very much for that reminder, Jenny. My body tells me that every morning." I held out the coffee cup. "How about filling this up again? I need all the caffeine I can get."

"I'll trade you fresh coffee for details of the reunion," Jenny said. "Not the sanitized version, either. The real story. And, by the way, Mark says no crime was committed. Your classmate committed suicide. He doesn't understand why you won't accept that."

"Is that why you're really here this morning, Jenny?" I asked. "To convince me that I'm wrong? That I should just let the whole thing drop?"

Another thought struck me with such force it took my breath away. "Did Mark send you to tell me to lay off? Not poke around? Is that why you're here?"

"Gosh, Mom, you're getting paranoid," Jenny said. "Can't your only daughter stop in for a quick cup of coffee and a chat with her mom without the mom going off the rails?

"Here." Jenny pushed a plate loaded with baked goods in my direction. "Have a bite of blueberry muffin. That'll cheer you up."

I did as Jenny suggested. Yes, I know, muffins have lots of fat and cholesterol, but they're one of my vices. After a few bites, I sighed in contentment. "Yummy. Thanks, sweetie. You're right. I do feel better. Almost human."

"Nothing like a quick combination of sugar and caffeine to make the world look brighter," Jenny said. "Now, I don't have to be on campus for an hour. Do you want to tell me everything that happened the night before the reunion? And," she looked at me, "what you're up to now. Because I know you're up to something. I can tell. I see the signs."

I shook my head. "No go, Jenny. I can't share with you this time. You'll say something to Mark and I'll be in hot water with the Fairport police. Again."

"Hey, Mom, that hurt," Jenny said. "I'm asking you to confide in Jenny-the-daughter, not Jenny-the-wife-of-a police-detective. You know it always helps for you to talk about things with me."

She narrowed her eyes and gave me a stare. "And if I know you, and I do, I bet you've already enlisted Mike to do some cyber sleuthing. Am I right?"

Trapped. That's what happens if you have a good relationship with your kids. One day, they grow up and know you better than you know yourself.

"Not one word about this to your husband," I said, wagging my index finger at her. "If I get in trouble with the police, I'll know who to blame."

"Cross my heart, Mom," Jenny said. "Unless you're about to confess that you're responsible for your classmate's death. Which is completely ridiculous. Now, talk."

So, I did. I went way back to the blue dress debacle, and how Meg bullied so many girls in our class and made their lives a misery. Even the ones we thought were her best friends. I told Jenny about how Meg had shown up and tried to take over the reunion planning, then stormed off in a huff when she couldn't get her own way. And relived the moment when Nancy and I walked into our room at Mount Saint Francis the night before the reunion and found her dead.

"Meg always claimed to be from a wealthy family," I continued. "And we believed her. But she lied about that. I don't know why that surprised me. But it did."

Then I told Jenny about the note the police found when Meg died, "Forgive me." "That's why Meg's death has been ruled a suicide," I said. "But I know, and lots of other people agree with me, that Meg was too vain to kill herself."

I took a deep breath. "Mary Alice and I spent yesterday afternoon at another classmate's house, Neecy Prentiss. It turns out that Meg's parents worked for her family. Meg's mother was the housekeeper, and her father took care of the grounds.

"Neecy admitted that she hated Meg. Even more than the rest of us did. Meg was really mean to her most of the time.

"Neecy ended up marrying Meg's old boyfriend, though."

I started to tell Jenny about the Tony-Neecy-Meg love triangle, but I realized her eyes had a glassy look.

Too much information, Carol. Cut to the chase.

"Neecy doesn't believe Meg killed herself, either. And she wanted to pay me to find out what really happened. She's afraid that, if it comes out how much she hated Meg, she'll be accused of her death."

You'll notice that I left out the part about the blackmail. I figured I'd ratted out Neecy enough without mentioning that. Nor did I mention *Fifty Shades of Navy*. No sense in confusing my daughter even more. Although I couldn't, for the life of me, figure out how that fit into the puzzle. And I was sure it did.

"I refused to take any money from Neecy," I said. "But I have asked Mike to see if he can find out what Meg's been up to for the forty years since we graduated. And I gave him a few more names to check out, too."

I frowned. "I should have given him J.T. Murray's name. I'll have to e-mail him and add that name to his list. J.T. is the director of marketing for Fairport Manor, the assisted living community. Which is what Mount Saint Francis Academy has become. I still can't quite believe that."

"Is J.T. a man or a woman?" Jenny asked. "There was a Jessica Murray who was a senior when Mark and I were freshman at Fairport High."

"A woman," I said. "I'm not sure how old she is."

"Let me think a minute," Jenny said. "Something terrible happened in that class. I think a student died."

She took a sip of her coffee and appeared lost in thought. "I remember now. One of the boys in that class died of a drug overdose right before graduation. He was Jessica's boyfriend. His name was Anthony something or other. I'm sorry. I can't remember his last name."

"It wasn't Prentiss, was it?" I asked.

"Yes, that's it," Jenny said. "Anthony Prentiss."

Chapter 36

For your information, I am the trophy wife. I just need a little more polishing than some of the newer models.

After Jenny left for school, I sat and pondered this new piece of information and tried to decide how important it was. After all, I already knew that J.T. worked at Fairport Manor, and Tony Prentiss was her boss. I wondered how accurate Jenny's account of the long-ago romance and subsequent tragedy was. Because she was only a freshman at the time, neither J.T. nor Anthony were in her immediate circle of friends.

Since Jenny and Mark were both freshmen in the same high school class, I reasoned that he must have heard about the tragedy, too. But maybe he didn't factor it in when he was investigating Meg's death.

Well, why would he? Mark was a trained police detective, used to dealing with cold, hard facts to solve a crime. Or a non-crime, as he termed Meg's death.

And Mark was a man.

Whereas I, as a woman and an incurable romantic, had absolutely no trouble concocting another Romeo and Juliet scenario for the J.T. Murray/Anthony Prentiss relationship.

"What if J.T. never got over losing Anthony?" I asked Lucy and Ethel. I sighed. "I guess this is one time when neither of you can relate to what I'm talking about. You've never been in love."

In my next life, maybe I'll become a fiction writer. After all, like most clever wives, I've been shading the truth for years.

This thought process, for some reason, brought me back to *Fifty Shades of Navy,* knee socks, and *Over The Knee Socks* – one of the catchy chapter titles I'd discovered during my late night e-book sleuthing.

Yuck.

Just thinking about that title made my blueberry muffin threaten to pay an unwanted return visit to my mouth.

I didn't want or need to read the book. I just needed to find out who the mysterious *Fifty Shades* author was. Later today, I'd concentrate on that.

Maybe.

But first, thanks to Jenny's tip, I did have something concrete to research – the death of Anthony Prentiss. I wondered if I could find an old obituary online. I had to figure out what year he died, though.

I was momentarily stumped, until I remembered that he was a senior at Fairport High School the year that Jenny and Mark were freshman. I did a quick Internet search, and found out that *The Fairport News,* our local weekly newspaper, archives obituaries going back twenty years. I figured that Anthony's death would have gotten huge coverage, since his family was so prominent in town.

Naturally, being me, when I went on the newspaper website, I got temporarily sidetracked by stories about other local events. I was particularly amused by the coverage of a long-ago town council meeting, when one Fairport resident threatened to punch out the First Selectman if he didn't permit dogs on our local beaches for part of the year.

Quickly, I scanned the fine print for the resident's name, and was relieved to see it wasn't anyone I knew. Like my husband, for instance.

Focus, Carol. You can come back to the site and entertain yourself some other time. Right now, you have a job to do.

I finally found what I was looking for. It was brief and to the point.

Anthony Prentiss, Jr., 18, died at his home on Tuesday. He was the beloved son of Anthony Prentiss, Sr., and Denise Nolan Prentiss. There will be no calling hours. Burial will be private.

I sat back in my chair and thought about what I'd read. And, perhaps more important, what I hadn't read.

How did Neecy and Tony go on after such a horrific loss? I'd be in grief therapy for the rest of my natural life.

"I wonder if J.T. had a chance to say goodbye," I said to the girls. "What if she had a complete breakdown when Anthony died?"

I had to talk this over with someone wiser than me, which describes most people I know. A person who would share a terrible burden without question, give sage advice if asked, and, above all, would never, under any circumstances, betray a confidence.

Not my hairdresser, Deanna, whom I frequently turn to when I'm in a muddle. I was going to a high authority.

I switched off the computer and headed for the shower. I would figure this out. Not by myself, of course. But I knew what my next step had to be.

So, after the dogs had been fed and exercised, I loaded them into the tailgate of my Jeep along with a bag of clothing to donate, and headed in the direction of the thrift shop.

And Sister Rose. Again.

Chapter 37

I shop, therefore I am. Broke.

"We only accept donations through the rear door of the shop," said the volunteer at the cash register. She gave me a look that made me feel like I'd committed a major crime. "You'll have to leave and come in through the back door. That's our policy. No exceptions."

"I'm a personal friend of Sister Rose," I said, not even giving the woman a passing glance as I steamrolled my way, lugging my bag of clothing, toward the back room of the thrift shop.

"I'm sure she won't mind my coming in the main entrance with donations," I called over my shoulder.

In a flash, the volunteer was beside me. "You can't go back there. Don't you see the sign on the door? It says, 'No admittance. Authorized personnel only.' What's the matter? Can't you read?"

Well! It had been a long time since I'd been treated this rudely.

"As a matter of fact, I read very well," I informed the woman. "Especially since Sister Rose was one of my teachers at Mount Saint Francis Academy. Excuse me."

And I pushed open the rear door to the sorting room, leaving the volunteer standing there on the other side.

"Carol, you're the answer to a prayer," Sister Rose said, greeting me with an unprecedented hug.

"I guess there's a first time for everything," I said. "But you might try telling your gatekeeper" – I gestured toward the front of the shop – "to be a little more welcoming. She almost bit my head off because I had the nerve to bring my donations in by the front door."

"It's Julie's first day," Sister Rose said. "And I'm afraid she's feeling overwhelmed. All the other volunteers I had scheduled called in sick. There's some sort of flu bug going around. And I can't stay in the front to train her properly, because I have to deal with all of these." She gestured around the floor of the shop, which was stacked with a variety of shopping bags and boxes. "Everyone in Fairport who doesn't have the flu must have decided to clean out their house today and bring us their donations. I can't keep up with it.

"That's why you're the answer to a prayer, Carol," Sister Rose continued. "You can stay today and help, can't you?"

"Well, I did come to talk to you for a quick minute. I hadn't planned on staying."

Nor did I really want to.

"And I have Lucy and Ethel in the car. They'll need to be exercised, and they'll need water, too."

You knew this would happen. Sister Rose always ropes you in to help her when you pop into the shop.

Oh, what the heck. All those bags to go through. Who knew what treasures I'd unearth? I wasn't brave enough to refuse Sister Rose, or suggest that she make an effort to recruit new volunteers for the shop. Lots of them.

Instead I sighed, put on my purple volunteer apron, and got to work. The questions would have to wait.

Fortunately, I am a multi-tasker. I can talk and sort at the same time. In fact, Jim claims that I can talk under any circumstances. I'm not exactly sure what he means by that, but I choose to take it as a compliment.

"So where are you with your sleuthing, Carol?" Sister Rose asked as we began sorting through another bag of donated clothing.

Boy, did that catch me off-guard.

"I was wondering how to start the conversation with you, Sister," I said. "But, as usual, you're way ahead of me."

Fortunately, Sister Rose didn't voice what I knew she was thinking – that she was always way ahead of me. Except in jumping to conclusions. I am the undisputed champion in that department.

I filled Sister Rose in on the visit to Neecy yesterday, and the surprising admission about her true relationship with Meg.

"But Neecy must have had some kind feelings toward Meg," Sister Rose pointed out. "Especially if she asked her to be her son's godmother. That's not a responsibility to be offered to just anyone."

"That was her parents' idea," I explained. "And Neecy said that Meg attended Anthony's funeral just to ask for money. Apparently, she asked Neecy for money several other times, too. And Neecy always gave it to her.

"And then, Meg showed up on Neecy's doorstep before our class reunion and expected a warm welcome. I can't imagine anyone else having that kind of nerve."

"Perhaps Meg came back to Fairport to apologize to all the people she'd wronged in the past," Sister Rose suggested. "Starting with Neecy and her husband. And then, she was overcome with her guilt. So she committed suicide on the eve of the class reunion. Remember, the note that was found next to her said, 'Forgive me.' "

It sounded plausible. If I didn't know Meg as well as I did, I could almost force myself to believe it.

But I didn't. Not for one second.

"Neecy doesn't believe that Meg committed suicide," I said. "And she's worried that, if the police figure out how much she hated Meg, she'll be accused of her death.

"I know this doesn't make any sense," I said, heading off Sister Rose's objections before she could voice them, "but I don't think Neecy is very stable, Sister. She's not thinking rationally. She's trying hard to support her husband in his election campaign, too. I'm sure that's causing even more stress for her. "

Sister Rose gave me one of her famous icy stares – the kind she used to give me in English class when I'd turned in a less than stellar homework assignment. "Then it's time for you to stop, Carol. By asking questions about Meg's death, you're causing innocent people a lot of unnecessary heartache."

Her expression softened. "I'm sure you don't want to do that."

"But Sister Rose," I said, stung by her criticism, "even though Neecy's terrified that Meg's death wasn't suicide, she wants to know the truth. In fact, she offered to pay me to find out.

"Of course, I refused," I said. "But if we don't find out what really happened, Neecy is always going to be afraid of being blamed for Meg's death. Don't you see? I have to keep going."

I wasn't sure if this train of thought made sense to Sister Rose. But it made sense to me. I was the one who saw how upset Neecy was yesterday.

"Poor Neecy," Sister Rose said. "She's such a lovely girl. I don't think she's been the same since her son died."

"I'm not asking questions to stir up trouble or heartache for anyone, Sister," I insisted. "Just the opposite. For some reason, people feel safe talking to me. And, not to brag, but I have been lucky enough to put a few puzzle pieces together and help the police solve a crime or two."

"You've been lucky, yes, but you also have a great deal of good old-fashioned common sense," said Sister Rose. "You are, after all, a Mount Saint Francis girl. I hope we trained you to think before you act, though. I do worry about that, dear."

Wow. A compliment, sort of, from Sister Rose. Nancy, Claire and Mary Alice would be very impressed. And, even more, surprised.

"All right, go ahead with your questions. But be careful. Don't ask questions willy nilly." Sister Rose smiled. "I don't think I've used that expression in years. I'll help you if I can. And please, keep me informed on what you're doing. I don't want any unpleasant surprises at my age."

Since Sister Rose was only a few years older than I was, I chose to ignore that comment.

"I agree with you that Neecy has been in a deep depression since her son, Anthony, died in his senior year of high school," I said. "My daughter Jenny told me this morning that J. T. Murray was Anthony's high school sweetheart. Jenny was a freshman at Fairport High School when Anthony and J. T. were seniors.

"J.T. is the now the marketing manager for Fairport Manor," I said, in case Sister Rose hadn't made the connection. "It seems very coincidental to me."

"I know who you mean, Carol," Sister said. She shook her head and stood, bringing our brainstorming session to an abrupt close.

"I hope you figure out how all these pieces fit together, Carol. But in the meantime, we'd both better get back to work." Sister Rose pointed to a cart that was overloaded with boxes of books. "This is a terrible job, but would you please sort and price this donation? Then I'd appreciate it if you could shelve the books according to fiction and nonfiction. We don't divide them any more than that. Oh, and please separate the hard covers from the paperbacks, too. Ask Julie to help you if she's not busy with a customer. Who knows? You might find a first edition or something else of value. It does happen."

Sister Rose opened the door to the sales floor, and the cart and I were summarily dismissed.

Have you ever been in the grocery store and had a shopping cart that had a will of its own? You know, one whose wheels refuse to go the way you want? Or, even worse, lock when you're trying to push it?

Imagine a flat, double-decker cart, laden with books of all shapes and sizes, slipping and sliding all over the place, that persisted in veering to the left, no matter how hard I tried to control it. And the darn thing squeaked, too.

I figured Sister Rose must have gotten the cart as a donation. No way would she have paid any money for it. I hoped the donor didn't get a tax receipt.

It was no wonder that, when I tried to turn the cart and push it up the ramp onto the main selling floor of the thrift shop, the cart stopped completely. And tipped over. Spilling books all over the floor.

I was reminded of the old saying, "No good deed ever goes unpunished." I was certainly being punished today.

"I wonder if Sister knows how dangerous this contraption is," I grumbled as I scrambled to pick up books as fast as I could and stack them on the cart in some semblance of order. "I'm lucky I didn't hurt somebody."

The volunteer cashier – Sister Rose said her name was Julie – hurried over to give me a hand, clearly demonstrating that she felt I was unable to handle the job on my own. At least, that's how I interpreted her unasked-for assistance.

"I've got this under control," I snapped. Then, I remembered my manners. "Thanks anyway."

"I just don't want Sister Rose to get angry," Julie said. Her eyes filled up – an automatic response I could completely identify with. "I've already jammed the cash register a couple of times and had to call her to help. She was not pleased."

"Hey, you're a volunteer," I assured her, forgiving Julie's earlier rudeness since I now understood the reason behind it. "Don't worry about it. Sister's under a lot of pressure, because the shop is so short-staffed today. Believe me, her bark is a lot worse than her bite. And she's a lot mellower now than she was when I had her as my English teacher."

"My mother had her in class, too," Julie said. "Fortunately, I was spared. I went to public school.

"Oh, no offense," she said, realizing how her remark sounded.

"None taken," I assured her, holding onto the cart and pulling myself to a standing position. "There. All the books are back on the cart. Now, if you'll just give it a boost, I think I can get the cart up the ramp and push it to the book section."

"Wait," said Julie. "You forgot one. This was under the front wheel." She handed me a bright yellow coil-bound notebook, the kind that we used in high school about a thousand years ago.

I looked at the notebook. "Property of The Golden Circle Club," the cover announced. "No Peeking. Private. Very Very Private."

I opened it. And found, scrawled in variety of penmanship styles, a series of diary entries titled, "How I Survived M.S.F.A.: The Tricks Of My Trade. Volume 2." Complete with a few diagrams that I...well. My goodness.

I snapped that book shut before Julie could take a quick gander at it.

I had another title for this notebook: *Fifty Shades of Navy – The Prequel!*

Chapter 38

I tell my husband all my secrets,
because he never listens to a thing I say.

I jammed the notebook in my apron pocket as fast as I could. I could feel my cheeks flame. My apron pocket felt like it was on fire, too.

I made a snap decision – I would not let Sister Rose see this notebook. It would only upset her. Or make her angry. I'd take it home when my volunteer shift was over and try to decipher the handwriting. And see if my instant assessment was correct.

But I knew I was right. Someone involved in this diary had to be the same mysterious person who wrote that filthy book. And that's why Sister Rose received an advance copy for comment. The author was a Mount Saint Francis girl.

All of these thoughts flashed through my mind in a nanosecond. Time to get back to work.

Act natural, Carol.

As if!

Julie looked at me curiously, and I managed a small smile. "Sister Rose asked me to sort the books, too, before I priced and shelved them. This one should be tossed, so I separated it out right away. I guess we need to find another place to put the discards." I laughed. Feebly. "My apron pocket isn't that big."

This was not one of my best on-the-spot explanations – I'm usually much more creative – but fortunately, Julie went along with it without question.

"I think you have a customer," I said, pointing in the direction of the check-out counter. *Thank God.*

"Oops! I better take care of this sale or Sister'll have my head." And Julie scurried away.

Phew. Saved by the cash register. And for once, it didn't cost Jim a single cent.

I think clearly when I'm driving. Some people (not mentioning anyone specific, understand) have been known to suggest that I should drive more often. Until the price of gas sky-rocketed.

Anyway, when I'm in the car, I can talk to myself without interruption, cry if I feel like it, or sing at the top of my lungs if a song comes on that I like. I bet you do some of those things, too. Of course, I have to be careful I don't get so distracted that I'm not paying attention to my driving. We "mature" drivers have a bad enough reputation as it is.

Especially since my license plate is not unknown to the Fairport police. Thanks to my son-in-law being on the force, lest you mistake my meaning.

The long shadows on Fairport Turnpike reminded me that the sun would be setting within the next hour. I hate it when the days get short and we lose daylight so early.

I wanted my house to be empty, so that I could go through the notebook without having to explain to You Know Who what I was doing. But, of course, that was not going to happen.

My heart sank when I saw Jim's car parked in front of the garage. He was home and, no doubt, hungry. No, scratch that. He was home and ravenous. And hell has no fury like a ravenous husband who has to wait for his dinner.

I debated the merits of a quick drive to Seafood Sandy's for a takeout meal. Nah, no time. Better to go in and see what I could whip up from the refrigerator.

To my complete surprise, my husband was dressed in a suit and tie, fresh from the shower, and greeted me with a big hug. Hmm. What had he been up to today?

And what was he up to now?

"I've fed the dogs, Carol, and they've run around the yard for half an hour."

Jim made a big show of looking at his watch. "You have exactly thirty minutes to shower and change. Wear something a little dressy. I love the way you look in that slinky red dress."

He wiggled his eyebrows. "I should tell you things like that more often.

"And then we have to leave. We don't want to be late."

"Late? Late for what? Where are we going?"

I took a closer look at my husband. He was looking pretty smug, all right. And in all the years we've been married, he's never told me what to wear. Sometimes, I think he doesn't even notice.

He notices the bills for my clothes, of course.

"I took the campaign mailing over to Tony Prentiss's election headquarters this morning," Jim said. "I had a chance to catch up with him. I hadn't seen him in years – not since high school. And he was nice enough to give us two comp tickets to a big fundraising shindig his committee is throwing at Westfair Country Club tonight. I didn't warn you in advance. I wanted to see the look on your face when I told you we were going to rub elbows with local high society tonight. You always say you have no excuse to get dressed up since I retired and we don't go to any fancy New York City parties anymore. Are you surprised?"

Surprised? Heck, yes.

I forgot all about the notebook. And that I really needed to check my e-mail to see how Mike was doing with his Internet sleuthing.

Instead, I worried that I'd never get the zipper to close on that darn red dress.

Rats.

"Wow, this sure is a crowded party," I said, clutching Jim's arm as we threaded our way across the ballroom of the Westfair Country Club. "Who are all these people? Do you think they'll all vote for Tony Prentiss on election day? If they do, he'll win by a landslide."

"Some people can't resist the lure of free food," Jim said. "For all I know, Tony is paying for this party himself. After all, he comped us."

"That's because we helped him out with the mailing," I reminded him as I looked around the room. "This is exciting. I've never been to a big political event before."

Jim squeezed my arm. "I see a few people I need to talk to. For the newspaper. Why don't you mingle for a few minutes? I'll be back."

And just like that, I was all by my lonesome. Just like at a high school mixer, when nobody asked me to dance.

Lordy, you are pathetic, Carol. Grow up and get yourself a white wine spritzer. At least that'll give you something to hold in your hands.

I was painfully aware that the red dress I had on – per my husband's request – was a little tighter than it had been the last time I'd worn it. So I avoided the siren call of the hors d'oeuvres, which looked delicious but loaded with calories I didn't need, and headed across the room to join the long line snaking toward the bar.

And nearly collided with my classmate, Mary Beth, who was headed in the same direction. "Carol!" she exclaimed. "I didn't expect to see a friendly face. Thank God."

"It's good to see you, too," I said, realizing that we hadn't talked since the reunion. And finding Meg's body.

"I'm here to support Neecy," Mary Beth said. "She asked me to come. She really hates these things, but she comes for Tony. You know how it is, when your husband is into something he thinks is so important. A wife's gotta do what a wife's gotta do, right?"

"I guess," I said halfheartedly. "I don't know how well I'd deal with the spotlight if Jim decided to run for office."

I looked around the crowded room. "Where is Neecy, anyway? Is she here?"

"She and Tony usually make a grand entrance at these bashes," Mary Beth said. "After most of the guests have had a chance to sample the food and have some wine. But, take it from me, the appetizers are the best part. Once we sit down to dinner, it'll be rubber chicken and peas for everyone."

I laughed. "Thanks for the tip. You can tell that I've never been to one of these things before, right? I'm glad I have you to show me the ropes. Since my dear husband seems to have gone temporarily AWOL."

The line inched forward toward the bar. And I suddenly realized I'd been given a golden opportunity (sorry about the pun) to quiz a classmate about the yellow notebook I'd found at the shop.

"I was at the thrift shop today," I said. "I stopped in with a box of donations, and Sister Rose grabbed me. You know how persuasive she can be."

Mary Beth laughed. "Do I ever! I try not stop in unless it's my regular weekly shift. She always gets me to stay." We made mindless small talk until we finally found ourselves at the head of the line.

"This one is on me," Mary Beth said, handing me a white wine spritzer with lots of ice. "I remember that you only drink spritzers. Which is probably smart. I like red wine, myself." She ordered a brand that I'd never heard of, gave the young bartender $30, and told him to keep the change. I was impressed.

"That's a pretty big tip," I said.

"I used to be a bartender myself in my younger days," Mary Beth said. "Some people are really stingy tippers. I try my best to make up for them."

"You won't believe what came into the thrift shop today," I said, taking a sip of my spritzer and trying to look casual.

Mary Beth laughed. "I've seen my share of surprises over the years," she said. "Like the old cloth purse that came in from an estate sale, and we found five hundred dollars hidden in a secret compartment. Sister Rose was thrilled about that. So, what did you find today?"

"Sister gave me a few boxes of donated books to sort, price and shelve." I said. "And when I was going through one of the boxes, I found a yellow notebook with the Mount Saint Francis logo on it. Remember those? The nuns used to dole them out to us every fall, so we could keep track of our classes."

"You mean you found somebody's old school notes?" Mary Beth said. "What a hoot. Too bad you didn't find them before the reunion. We all could have had a good laugh."

"It wasn't exactly class notes" I said, my cheeks burning at the memory. "Have you ever heard of something called The Golden Circle Club? I took the notebook home to try to decipher it."

"Never heard of it," Mary Beth said, a little too quickly.

"Oh, look, here come Tony and Neecy. I'm going to the front of the room so she can see me. Bye, Carol. It was nice chatting with you."

And, just like that, she melted into the crowd. I didn't even get the chance to ask her if she knew about J.T. Murray and Anthony Prentiss.

Chapter 39

Come rain or come shine, I never lose my taste for whine.

"That was fun," I said, leaning back against the headrest in Jim's car and sighing with contentment. "Although, if I never go to a political fundraiser again, that's ok with me."

"The food was pretty bad," Jim said. "Except for the hors d'oeuvres." He gave me a sidelong glance. "Which I saw you sampling a few times."

I pulled down the skirt on my tight red dress. And ignored my husband's comment.

"I ran into a high school classmate of mine, Mary Beth Walsh," I said. "She tipped me off that the hors d'oeuvres were the best part of the meal, and urged me to fill up. So, I did."

I turned to glare at my spouse, although I doubted that he could see me in the dark. "You were no help. You left me standing there all by myself. Thank you very much."

"We sat together at dinner," Jim said, sounding a wee bit defensive. "I made every effort to find you in the crowd."

"Eventually," I said, not willing to give him an inch. "But I forgive you. After all, this is the closest we've gotten to a date in months."

The motion-sensitive lights went on as we crossed the yard toward the side door. The kitchen was ablaze with light. Lights that I had not turned on before we left for the fundraiser. And which were not on a timer.

I stopped and grabbed my husband's arm. "Jim. I think someone's been in the house. Oh, my God, the dogs!"

Of course, I had overreacted. I bet you're not surprised about that. Lucy and Ethel were fine. For some reason, though, they were locked in our bedroom, and complaining at the top of their lungs.

"You must have closed them inside when we left," Jim said, patting my arm. "And didn't realize it. You know how sneaky they can be. They were probably playing with a toy under the bed, and you didn't know it. I've checked all around the house, and nothing's been disturbed. And I'll bet you left the kitchen lights on, too. We did leave in a hurry.

"You know, Carol, at our age, we tend to be forgetful."

He gave me a big smooch. "It was a fun night. Are you coming to bed now?"

I didn't want to argue with Jim, but I was positive I hadn't locked the dogs in the bedroom. Nor had I left the lights on in the kitchen. He was right, though – nothing had been touched. So I did my best to convince myself that he was right. The other possibility was too scary for me to think about.

I was still jumpy. And not at all ready for sleep.

"You know, Jim, I think I'll stay up a little while and read. I'll try not to wake you when I come to bed," I said. Not that I ever have. After thirty-plus years of marriage, my track record in that department remains unblemished.

The yellow notebook I planned to read would probably keep me awake for hours, but now was as good a time as ever. Especially after Mary Beth's odd reaction to my Golden Circle Club question. She had piqued my curiosity even more, and I hoped I might recognize the handwriting in the infamous notebook.

Jim gave me another smooch – this fundraiser was paying off big-time for me – and headed toward the bedroom.

I walked the dogs in the yard – on leashes, just to be sure – then fixed myself a cup of warm milk. Time to check that notebook and see if I could make any sense of it. And check in with Mike via the computer.

I tried to ignore the funny feeling I had that someone had been in my house. Jim had checked every room, and all was well.

I went into the office and rummaged on my desk for the yellow notebook. Which I was positive I had left there. In plain sight. Before we left for the fundraiser.

It was gone.

I never understood that old expression, "a prickle of fear." Until that instant. My whole body was prickling.

I immediately jumped up and turned on every light in the house except our bedroom. I felt a little safer.

But not much.

Lucy and Ethel, thinking that morning had come extra early in the Andrews house, which therefore meant food service for them, padded into the office and sat at my feet. Looking hopeful.

Just seeing them made me feel better. Although I was a little angry with them, too. Some watchdogs they'd turned out to be.

"Gosh, I wish you two could talk," I said, getting down on the floor and nuzzling them close. Lucy gave me a reproachful look, telegraphing that they did so many other things to communicate with me, talking aloud was totally unnecessary.

I just had to pick up the obvious clues they were giving me.

"What should I do?" I asked them. "Should I call the police?" Even Ethel raised her doggy eyebrows at that idea.

"You're right," I said. "After all, there's no sign of a break-in, and nothing was taken except the stupid notebook. And I'm the only one who's ever seen the darn thing. They'll think I'm nuts."

Lucy refrained from comment. And stared at the computer.

"I guess I've seen enough of the book to make a few notes," I said, following her gaze. "Good idea. And I can see what Mike's come up with, too."

Satisfied that they had done enough to save me from making a fool of myself with the police, and pointed me in the correct direction, the dogs curled up at my feet. In about a second, both were snoring.

Being bossy tires them out. Me, too.

I scrunched my eyes and tried to remember what the handwriting I'd seen in the notebook looked like. But it was no use. I'd only glanced at the pages for a second, realized what I was looking at, and slammed the book shut.

"I wish I had another way to check out the Golden Circle Club," I said to myself in frustration. "But I have no idea how." I looked at Lucy, who had raised her head and was giving me a dirty look. "Sorry I woke you, Lucy," I said. "I'll whisper from now on."

Lucy rose, gave a deep sigh, then arched and stretched her back. I envied her. If I tried that pose, I'd end up at the chiropractor for sure.

She walked over to the built-in bookcase on the opposite side of the room, sat down, and stared. Then she turned around, gave me another stare, and turned back to the bookcase again.

And, all of a sudden, I saw what she was looking at. My high school yearbook! And she was absolutely right. Because if such a club existed at Mount Saint Francis while I was in school there, it would be mentioned in our yearbook.

"Lucy, you are so smart," I said. "Thanks. You've saved me a lot of time."

Lucy gave me one last stare, yawned, and went back to cuddle with Ethel and catch some more sleep. And I got the message. *That's it for tonight, Carol. No more clues. Now, let me get some rest.*

Swear to God, that's what she said.

I hadn't looked at the yearbook for years. Nancy had brought hers to one of our reunion planning meetings, but I didn't bother to check it out. She even suggested that we have miniature ones made and put at each person's place for the lunch, but the rest of us nixed that idea right away. It was bad enough to wear a reunion nametag that sported our high school graduation picture. A most humbling experience.

I found a comfortable position on the sofa and leafed through the first few pages. Hmm. I had forgotten that Mary Beth was the yearbook editor. I was on the writing staff, naturally, but she was the big boss. And she really ran the whole show, now that I thought about it. Our advisor, Sister Dorothea, had a health issue midway through senior school year which forced her to lighten her school responsibilities, including overseeing the contents of our yearbook.

I skimmed the individual pictures – although I did stop on page 32 and stare for a quick minute at a geeky-looking girl with a bouffant hairdo who looked like she was a refugee from a windstorm.

Thank goodness I went to Deanna now for my hairstyling. That bouffant was too much, in every way!

I tore through the book as fast as I could until I got to the extracurricular activities section. Home Ec, History, Latin (yes, we did take that in high school), French, Spanish, Drama, English, Glee Club, and on and on. And there it was – the very last one. The Golden Circle Club. There were only five members, which was odd because most of the clubs had at least 20. In fact, if I remembered correctly, in order to be recognized as an official school club, that was a requirement.

The five members of the Golden Circle Club were pictured holding a notebook that looked exactly like the one I'd found at the thrift shop. The three Marys, Neecy, and the person who was definitely the leader of this unlikely group, with a huge smirk on her face.

Meg.

I was betting that the good sisters at Mount Saint Francis had absolutely no idea what extracurricular activities this particular club encouraged. And I was sure that, if Mary Beth hadn't been the editor, this picture never would have made it into our yearbook at all.

Chapter 40

One secret for aging gracefully is to lie about your age. Add 10 years and everyone will tell you how great you look.

I put my head back on the sofa – just for a minute, to rest my eyes – and thought about what I'd learned. I realized I hadn't found out anything I hadn't suspected before. But my suspicions had been confirmed.

I knew that it was a huge leap from a yellow notebook detailing the risqué off-campus adventures in a 1970s Catholic girls' high school to writing a best-selling mommie porn book. But I also knew that if anyone had the anatomy required to get the job done (you can fill in whatever body parts you deem appropriate here), it would have been Meg.

This was a no-brainer. Especially for me and my overactive imagination. But convincing other people – say, my son-in-law the Fairport detective – that this was the motive for Meg's untimely death would be a lot harder. And the idea that four of my very own classmates were responsible, well, that was a stretch, even for me.

Even though I couldn't ignore the coincidence between my asking Mary Beth about the Golden Circle Club and the immediate theft of the yellow notebook.

Although I never saw Mary Beth leave the fundraiser for more than five minutes. She couldn't have gotten to my house and back in that short amount of time.

Unless she sent someone else. But who?

Blast. I knew I was onto something, but it still wasn't clear.

I still needed more information on how Meg had spent the intervening forty years between high school graduation and our reunion. And her death.

The clock on the computer reminded me that it was now way past midnight. If I was going to stay up any later, I'd need a shot of caffeine. And then I'd never get to sleep at all.

I decided to check my e-mails one last time and then head off to bed. Tomorrow was another day, as Scarlet O'Hara would say. Or did she say that she'd never be hungry again? Either phrase worked for me.

Instant message from Nancy:

R U up? I can't sleep.

Me: *Me neither.*

Nancy: *Y?*

Me: *Ever heard of the Golden Circle Club?*

Nancy: *Call me on my cell right away.*

My BFF didn't give me a chance to punch in her cell number. In a millisecond my own phone rang – I'd had the foresight to keep it with me in case Mike and I needed to talk. An unusual step for me to be so organized, but I'm trying.

"Carol!" Nancy screeched at me. "It's me."

"I know, Nancy," I said. "I have caller ID. Why do we have to talk now? What's so urgent that it can't wait until morning." I yawned loudly, for effect. "I'm beat. I need to go to bed."

"You won't want to go to bed when you hear what I've got to tell you," Nancy said, sounding a little calmer now. "How did you hear about the Golden Circle Club? I haven't thought about it in forty years. If the nuns had found out about it, I bet some girls would have been expelled. Or, at least, suspended."

"How come you know about this and I don't?" I asked.

"You talk first," Nancy said. "I'm not telling you anything until you level with me about what you've heard."

This was very frustrating. Usually Nancy was willing to share anything with me. Too much, actually.

But since I wasn't going to get anywhere until I spilled what I knew, I filled Nancy in about the find at the thrift shop, what I'd gleaned from my quick scanning of the notebook, my questioning of Mary Beth and checking out our yearbook. I finished by telling Nancy that the notebook was now gone, and I was sure someone had come into my house and taken it.

But I had no proof. (Not that that's ever stopped me before, mind you.)

I resisted drawing a parallel with *Fifty Shades of Navy*, deciding to see if Nancy jumped to the same conclusion all on her own.

When I was finished, I heard only silence on the other end of the phone. It was so long that I thought Nancy had either hung up or the connection had been broken.

Then, a deep sigh.

"All right, Carol, I'll tell you what I know. But you're not going to believe me."

"Try me," I said.

"The Golden Circle Club started sophomore year at Mount Saint Francis. It was a secret club, and membership was by invitation only. I bet you can guess whose idea it was without my telling you."

"Meg's, of course," I said.

"One hundred percent correct," said Nancy.

"Anyway, the original idea behind it was that each month one member had to do something completely outrageous. It was done by rotation. And report back to the club at the next meeting about what she had done. And bring some sort of proof that she'd actually done what she claimed she did. Does this make sense?"

I nodded. Then I realized that Nancy couldn't see me, so I said, "So far."

"The first year, it was pretty innocent. Like smoking in the bathroom and leaving cigarette butts there for proof. The events were all documented in a yellow notebook. The scribe duty was done by rotation, too. But by junior year, Meg upped the ante and changed the focus. It became more…outrageous. Bordering on the illegal. And by senior year, well, I suspect that the notebook you found detailed some of those exploits. Although I'm pretty sure that a lot of those never really happened. They could have been copied from racy magazines or books."

Long pause on Nancy's end of the phone.

"Are you with me, Carol?"

"I guess."

"There was a signature cocktail that everyone had to drink at the meetings. It was something creamy and pink – I don't remember the name of it – but it packed a real wallop. Especially for girls who weren't used to drinking. Maybe there was even some pot smoking."

Nancy took a deep breath.

"I'm not proud of this, but I guess it's time to come clean with you. I was a member in sophomore year."

"What? You're not serious." I was shocked. Really shocked.

"I only stayed for a few months," Nancy said in her own defense. "Like I said, in the beginning, the pranks were no big deal. But then, they got more out of hand, and I left. But I had to swear I would never reveal anything about the club to anyone. Even to my closest friends."

"What about the notebook I found? Do you know anything about that?"

"We never meant anyone to see the notebooks," Nancy said. "I don't know who took them for safekeeping. Whoever it was should have burned the darn things."

"Isn't it odd how that notebook found its way into the thrift shop?" I said. "Maybe the universe is trying to tell us something."

Nancy sniffled. It sounded like she was crying, but didn't want me to know.

"I hope you don't hate me for this," she said. "Please don't let this ruin our friendship. You really are the very best friend I've ever had. Ever. And I love you."

"Oh, for heaven's sake," I said. "I don't hate you. You're my best friend and always will be. You did something really stupid when you were younger. When you realized what you'd gotten yourself into, you quit. But I don't understand why you got involved with that club in the first place, especially since you admitted how much you disliked Meg."

"I don't know why I did, either. I guess I thought it was exciting. And I was thrilled to be asked to join. At first."

I tried to focus on what Nancy had confessed to me. I was so exhausted by that time that curling up with Lucy and Ethel on the office floor looked like a great idea. Walking to the bedroom would be too much of an effort.

I think I nodded off for a split second, because I heard Nancy yelling my name from what seemed a faraway place.

Which was my office floor. I had dropped the phone.

"I'm here!" I said. "I'm thinking."

"I was worried. You were so quiet."

"I'm beat," I said. "And you've given me a lot to think about. But I'm too tired to think about anything now. I'm going to bed. I do have one question I want to ask you before I hang up, though. What would you do if you thought the Golden Circle Club secrets were about to become public knowledge?"

"I don't know what you're getting at," Nancy said

"If you'd stayed in the club all through high school, and gotten involved in some of the more dicey things, and hid it from everyone for your entire adult life, what would you do if you thought someone was going to spill the beans? Blow the whistle? Pick any phrase that you want."

"I guess I'd be upset and embarrassed about it," Nancy said. "I wouldn't like it at all. You're not going to tell anyone else what I told you, are you, Carol? Like Jim? Oh, God, please promise me you won't."

"Of course I won't, Nancy," I assured her. "This is your story, not mine."

We said our goodnights and I finally dragged my weary bones off to bed. I remember my last conscious thought, before I drifted off to sleep.

Would anyone kill to keep this secret?

Chapter 41

I'm not overweight. I'm undertall.

When I finally came to about five hours later, the sun was streaming in our bedroom window, reminding me yet again that my pathetic attempt at fall cleaning had better start with them. And soon.

I groaned and rolled over. I felt like someone had hit me over the head with a sledge hammer. There was a note pinned to Jim's pillow. "Off to have breakfast with Tony Prentiss. He's giving me an exclusive interview for next week's paper. For old times' sake. See you at dinner. I'll be home by five o'clock."

Tony Prentiss. The fundraiser. That darn yellow notebook. A possible break-in at our house.

And Nancy's late-night confession.

I squeezed my baby blues shut and willed myself back to sleep. This was one day I definitely did *not* want to face. Especially if it ended with some of my classmates being arrested for murder. Because of my overactive imagination and big mouth.

Lucy and Ethel had a different idea. One, then the other jumped onto the bed and started licking my face.

"Ok, girls, I'm getting up. But I hope you made the coffee."

As I was performing my regular morning ablutions, the rational side of my brain kicked in. Yes, believe it or not, I do have one.

I was going to take this so-called investigation very slowly. Not jump to conclusions, the way I always did. Because there probably were a million rational explanations for Meg's death. Maybe she was sick. Maybe she really did commit suicide, and wanted to do it at school, where she had spent so many happy years bossing the rest of us around. Or maybe she wanted to commit suicide so she could ruin our reunion, because she didn't get her own way about organizing it.

Nah, that last one was a stretch, even for me.

But Meg always wanted to be the center of attention. And the Boss Of All Bosses. Maybe this was her last, pathetic act to draw everyone's eyes to her. And she decided to do it in my room, as her parting shot.

Ok, maybe all of this was pretty feeble, but I had shown myself that there was more than one way to connect the dots. I just wasn't sure which way was the right one. Or if none of them was.

Feeling a little better, I pulled on a pair of Jim's old sweatpants and a baggy tee shirt and headed toward the kitchen. Forget about using meditation or yoga to calm the nerves. Self-delusion works much better for me.

Fortified by a cup of steaming coffee and a toasted English muffin (light on the butter, heavier on the marmalade), I discussed my plan of action with the dogs. They were in a very good mood and even more willing to listen than usual. I'd bribed them with extra kibble in their breakfast bowls this morning.

We all agreed that the first thing on my agenda should be checking to see if my darling son had uncovered anything juicy about any of the suspects. I mean, about my classmates.

And the victim, of course. Couldn't forget about Meg. In fact, every mystery I've ever read – probably hundreds of them over the years – suggest that the solution to a crime is often found by investigating the life and personality of the victim.

And investigating is a much more elegant word than snooping, don't you think?

I fired up my laptop and was delighted to see twelve different e-mails from Mike. He'd been a very busy boy, indeed.

I skimmed his reports on two of the Marys – Mary Catherine and Mary Ann. Typical middle class matron info – married to the same guy since college, a brief stab at a career but nothing serious, two kids each, very involved in school activities when kids were younger, yada yada yada. And never moved out of Fairport.

I yawned and stretched. What boring lives they'd had. Then, I realized that my life was exactly the same as theirs. And mine had been anything but boring.

Note to self: Stop being so critical of other people.

Mary Beth did a two-year stint interning at a New York public relations agency right after college. But then she left, got married, had one daughter, and settled down in Fairport.

Meg's profile was by far the most interesting. And, yes, mysterious. Over the past forty years she'd held a wide variety of jobs under an equal variety of different names.

Mike pointed out to me, in all capital letters, how hard it was to trace her.

This took me hours, Cosmo girl. I wouldn't have spent all this time on it for anyone else. And the fact that my current girlfriend dumped me the night before last, leaving me with an unexpected amount of free time, was purely coincidental. So don't go asking me any questions about my love life.

Well, of course, he was only doing that to tease me. Ring my chimes. Pique my insatiable curiosity. The little stinker. He knew that I'd suffer in silence and not cross-examine him about his latest romance as long as I had all this other information to sift through.

I was just starting to delve more into Meg's life history when Lucy ran to the side door and started to bark. Double rats. It was too early in the morning for anyone to expect a warm greeting from me.

So I ignored Lucy and continued to focus on my computer screen. Until I was disturbed by an insistent tapping at my office window. And a familiar face mouthing, "Let me in, Carol. It's cold out here."

It was Claire.

"You are just the person I needed to talk to," I said, pouring a cup of lukewarm coffee and nuking it in the microwave.

"I can see that," Claire said. "That's why you left me standing outside your house for such a long time."

I was embarrassed. Claire could always do that to me.

But I recovered quickly. "I haven't even showered yet," I shot back. "And I didn't know it was you. I was involved in solving my latest mystery. Meg's death."

That stopped Claire cold. As I knew it would. But not for long.

"What the heck are you talking about?" Claire demanded. "Did something else happen, or is this a case of your overactive imagination working overtime again?"

Well!

"Where've you been, anyway?" I asked, deciding to switch subjects and make her beg me for information. "The last I heard, you and Larry went to the Berkshires for a long weekend. You've been gone a lot longer than that."

"I know you're stalling me, Carol," Claire said. "But I'll play along. We did go the Berkshires, and then decided, on the spur of the moment, to fly to Florida and check our condo. We're going back right after Christmas this year, and expect to stay until April.

"And to answer your next two questions, Mary Alice is doing special duty at the hospital, and Nancy has a staff meeting at the real estate office. We just got back into town last night, and I'm trying to get caught up with everyone. You were the only one I could find at home."

She fixed me with a look that told me I better not stall any longer. "So, what's up, Carol? Apparently, I missed quite a lot while I was away."

"I'll fill you in," I said. "It'll take some time. And what I'm really hoping is that you'll tell me I'm crazy."

"Not a problem," said Claire. "I've had lots of practice doing that over the years. Now, talk."

I'm not going to bore you all with what you already know. And I admit that it takes me a lot longer to tell a story than most other people. I tend to digress.

Like I'm doing right now.

By the time I finished with Mary Alice and my visiting Neecy, Neecy's startling request, the Golden Circle Club and the notebook, the fundraiser and Mary Beth, my suspicions about a house break-in and the theft of the notebook, *Fifty Shades of Navy* and Mike's cyber sleuthing, plus Nancy's late night confession, I was exhausted.

Claire didn't interrupt me one single time. Which was surprising. She always tended to poke holes in my theories at every opportunity. Sort of like my personal devil's advocate.

"So, do you think I'm crazy, Claire? You won't hurt my feelings if you tell me that."

Much.

Claire sighed. "I wish I did, Carol. These women are our friends. But this time, I think you're onto something. We have to figure out what to do next."

I cocked my head and stared at my friend. "Did I hear you correctly? Did you say, 'we'?"

"Well, of course, silly. You don't think I'm going to let you solve this one without me, do you? Two heads are always better than one. And you tend to go off half-cocked most of the time and act before you think things through. I'm extra cautious, so I'll balance you out."

Claire closed her eyes and held up her hand for silence. "Let me think for a minute. What's the best way to do this?"

Her eyes snapped open. "Ok, I've got an idea. I think we should round up the usual suspects, like Poirot would do. And prod them a little bit with some of the information you've uncovered. See if one of them gets really upset. Or acts guilty."

"Claire, that's a nutty idea," I said. "If I came up with it, you'd shoot it right down. First of all, how are we going to get everyone together?

And how are we going to prod someone to 'confess,' as you so quaintly put it?"

"Getting them together is the easy part, Carol," Claire said. "We haven't had a reunion committee wrap-up meeting yet. That's a perfect excuse. So we'll invite Neecy, the three Marys, Sister Rose…"

"Come on, Claire, don't tell me you suspect Sister Rose!"

"Don't be ridiculous, Carol. But we'll need her here to keep things rolling along. Of course, we should clue her in ahead of time. And also Nancy and Mary Alice, naturally. We'll need to talk to them ahead of time, too."

"I think we should also invite J.T. Murray, the Fairport Manor marketing director," I said. "She was Anthony Prentiss's high school sweetheart. Oh, did I tell you about that part?"

"If you think she should be at the meeting, by all means, invite her," Claire said. "I don't think I can handle anymore information right now. My brain's on overload as it is."

"I'm having second thoughts about this," I said. "I don't want to insult anyone or hurt her feelings. Especially if I'm wrong."

Claire waved her hand. "Nonsense, Carol. We'll be subtle. And besides, you have to break a few eggs to make an omelet, right?"

"I guess. I'm still not sure if this is such a good idea, though. And where will we have the meeting?"

Claire looked at me in complete surprise. "I thought we'd have it here, Carol. In your dining room. Ok?"

I nodded with a total lack of enthusiasm. Now, I had to cook and clean, too, as well as solve a mystery.

Claire laughed. "I know what you're thinking, Carol. We'll all pitch in. You won't have to do much at all."

Fine by me.

"But I still don't see how you're going to get someone to confess, Claire."

"I have a yellow notebook from Mount Saint Francis, too," Claire said. "If you can remember exactly what the words were on the notebook you saw, I'll put them on the cover. And I'll add 'The Golden Circle Club' in big letters. I'm betting that, when the committee sees the notebook, someone will crack. Especially if the incriminating notebook was stolen from your house."

Claire patted my hand. "Don't worry, Carol. I'll take care of everything."

That's what I was afraid of.

Chapter 42

To paraphrase the late Wallis Simpson, Duchess of Windsor, a woman can never be too rich, too thin, or have too many dogs.

It took almost a week to come up with a date that the entire committee agreed to for our reunion wrap-up/murder interrogation meeting. Lordy, with all those e-mails and texts back and forth – and first one, then another of the Marys saying, "Oh, no that won't work for me. I have yoga that day," or some equally lame excuse – I was getting more and more hyper. And unsure of myself and my off-the-wall conclusions. Was it possible that these women really had such active lives, or did our suspects figure out that this meeting was about more than talking over whether we liked the reunion menu or the centerpieces?

And I wasn't sure exactly what was planned, either. For instance, who was going to run the meeting? Nancy was the self-appointed reunion chairperson, but Claire was the one who had cooked up this plan. And where did Sister Rose fit in? How much did she, or Mary Alice, know about why we were getting together?

I absolutely *hate* not being in control of a situation, especially in my own house, for Pete's sake. But I decided to make a Caesar salad, with sides of fresh shrimp and chicken so people could add them as desired, and bought a variety of fresh breads from The Paperback Café.

I am a salad maker, not a baker.

A simple lunch, but one that would fill people up. Depending on how much bread they consumed, of course.

Besides, if all went as we hoped, at least one person would be eating and running, so to speak, so I didn't want to serve anything that would get cold, like a quiche, for instance. I do try to plan ahead.

I wanted to serve a white wine along with coffee and tea and bottled water. But Claire vetoed that. She said she had her own little surprise for drinks.

Nancy was the first to arrive, and when she took her place at the head of the dining room table, I didn't even give her a dirty look. Although that should have been my seat.

One by one, the rest of the committee trickled in.

"It's so nice to get together, Carol," Mary Ann said, giving me a hug. "Thanks for hosting again. I feel like we're taking advantage of your hospitality."

"I'm glad to do it," I said, returning her hug. "And Jim always appreciates leftovers."

Sister Rose and Mary Alice arrived together, as did Mary Catherine and Mary Beth.

"J.T. may be a little late," Sister Rose explained. "I stopped by Mount Saint Francis..." she laughed and corrected herself, "I mean, Fairport Manor, to see if she wanted to carpool with us, but she was showing a prospective tenant around the property."

It suddenly hit me that Claire hadn't come yet. Where the heck was she? This was supposed to be her show. Now, I was really sweating this luncheon out, although I tried not to show it.

When Neecy arrived, she looked as nervous as I felt. So because I am such a super nice person, as well as a perfect hostess who always puts her guests at ease (even the ones suspected of murder), I suggested she bring Porter into the house to play with Lucy and Ethel.

All three canines, glad to be together again, took advantage of the situation – and me – by bounding into the dining room and saying their doggy hellos to all the guests, sniffing and nuzzling as they went.

I made a show out of shooing all three dogs back into the kitchen so I could put up a baby gate. We use the gate to keep the girls confined in the kitchen whenever we have guests – Lucy and Ethel are terrible beggars. I was stalling for time until Claire got here, and I knew the dogs were a great diversion.

I was just about to offer the guests a tour of my antique house – which shows how desperate I was, because I never do that! – when I heard the kitchen door slam. Claire poked her head around the corner of the dining room. "Sorry I'm late, everyone," she said, "but I had to make a few stops on my way. J.T. is just parking her car and then she'll be right in. Did I miss anything?"

I shot Claire a dirty look, telling her loud and clear that she better get in here and get this show started. Right now.

When Claire and J.T. – the latter looking very stressed – finally took their seats, Nancy cleared her throat and tapped on a water glass to stop the chatter.

"I want to thank everyone for all the hard work you did to make our Ruby Reunion such a fabulous event," she said. "I'm sure the class will be talking about it for years."

Well, sure they would. It wasn't every reunion that provided a dead body as one of the guests.

I didn't really say that. Of course.

"Not that the event was perfect. Meg's death was so tragic." Nancy shook her head. "I'll never understand why someone would take her own life. She must have been despondent, poor girl."

Nancy's eyes filled with tears. I always admired her ability to do that whenever she wanted. Her talent for whipping up tears got us out of a lot of tight spots when we were in school.

"The really sad thing, and I'm sure you'll all agree with me about this, is that we never had an opportunity to say goodbye, since I'm told that Meg has already been buried in upstate New York . So before we begin to eat the delicious lunch I know Carol has prepared, I've asked Sister Rose to lead us in a farewell tribute to our dear departed classmate."

Sister Rose took her place at the head of my dining room table and said, "Everyone, please close your eyes and bow your heads. We will now offer a prayer for the soul of the late Mary Margaret Mahoney."

As Sister Rose led the prayer, I snuck a quick peek and realized that the three Marys and J.T. not only had their eyes open, but they were all looking daggers at Sister Rose. Neecy had her head bowed but did not join in the prayer itself.

Interesting.

As if the prayer wasn't enough to make the entire room (including me) uncomfortable, Sister Rose upped the ante even more. "I think it would be appropriate for each of us who knew Meg so well to share a special memory of the deceased." Her message was clear: This is not a suggestion. You will all do it.

Sister Rose looked around the room. "Who would like to go first? How about you, Mary Ann?" Boy, this was just like being back at Mount Saint Francis when Sister Rose would give us a surprise pop quiz. Even Nancy's tears didn't get us out of those.

At that point, I escaped into the kitchen to get the salad for lunch. No way was I going to share anything, and being the nominal hostess did give me some privileges. Plus, being in the kitchen gave me a better opportunity to observe most of the suspects – I mean, my classmates – at one time.

And boy, were the Golden Circle girls wriggling in their seats.

I was fussing over the number of individual salad bowls to bring to the table – I know, I should have set the table before anyone arrived but I ran out of time – when I heard Claire call my name. Sticking my head around the doorway, I said, "I'll be in with lunch in a jiffy, Claire. But I could use a little help carrying things."

So get up, get out here, and tell me what's going on.

"Hold the salad for a sec, Carol, ok?" Claire said. "I think it's time for a toast. There's a pitcher in your refrigerator, on the second shelf. Would you bring that in, please?"

"Oh, sure. I'm on it."

Never mind the fact that this was *my* refrigerator in my kitchen in *my* home and Claire was treating me like I was the hired help instead of the lady of the house. That's what being a good sport is all about.

Claire had now taken Sister Rose's place at the head of *my* dining room table and gestured to me to bring the pitcher to her.

Gritting my teeth and reminding myself what we were here for – well, what some of us were here for, to solve the mystery of Meg's death – I resisted saying, "Yes, Your Majesty," and carefully placed the pitcher in front of Claire without spilling a single drop on my damask tablecloth.

"Everyone pass your glasses to me and I'll fill them up," Claire said. She proceeded to pour a creamy pink concoction that looked like Pepto-Bismol into each glass.

Mary Beth examined hers and asked, "What exactly is this? It looks like medicine."

"It's a drink recipe I happened across recently," Claire said. She raised her glass to begin the toast. "It's called a Pink Squirrel."

The three Marys choked.

"We drank these every time we got together for...." Neecy blushed as Mary Beth caught her eye. "Never mind. I think I'm remembering wrong."

"What should we drink to?" Sister Rose asked.

"How about to the reunion committee?" Mary Alice suggested. "And to departed friends."

I took a generous sip. Hey, I was entitled. I wasn't used to this much stress in my house. Especially stress that I wasn't responsible for.

Boy, I never knew that squirrels – pink ones, that is – packed such a punch in their cute little claws. This drink tasted as smooth as a milkshake, but when it hit the digestive system, look out. It was a good thing we were having lunch soon, to offset the effects of the alcohol.

By this time, Nancy had resumed her place at the head of the table. "Ok, people," she said, "it's time to get down to business before we have lunch. Let's talk about our reunion. How does everyone think it went?"

She colored slightly. "Apart from Meg's death, of course. I thought it was fabulous."

"I think it would be a good idea if someone took notes at this meeting." Mary Alice suggested. "After all, in five more years, we'll be planning another one." I shot her a look, and she immediately backtracked. "I mean, in five more years there'll be another reunion, but we won't necessarily be the ones planning it."

Nancy nodded her approval. "Great idea. Claire, would you please take notes? You always took the best ones in school."

"I'll be glad to, Nancy," said Claire. She whipped out a yellow coil-bound notebook imprinted with the Mount Saint Francis logo and the words "Golden Circle Club" on the cover.

And that's when all hell broke loose. No kidding.

I thought the three Marys would have heart attacks, right there in my dining room. Then, Mary Beth grabbed for the notebook, but missed.

Mary Ann grabbed the notebook from Claire and threw it to Mary Catherine. Mary Catherine lobbed it to Mary Beth, who threw it to Neecy. Neecy threw the notebook up in the air and narrowly hitting missed my Waterford chandelier. Then, she started to cry.

Porter, recognizing the sound of her mistress's sobbing, made a flying leap over the baby gate separating the kitchen from the dining room. She caught the notebook in mid-air, raced toward Neecy, and dropped the notebook in her lap like the good dog she was.

Hey, Porter's a Labrador Retriever, remember? So, she retrieved.

The three Marys all tried to make a break for my side door. But Mary Alice and Claire were too quick for them and blocked their exit.

The only one who didn't say a word through this entire thing was J.T., which I put down to the fact that she was too young to know what the notebook signified.

Sister Rose rapped on the table for silence. And, of course, got it. Then said, "I think someone here has something to say. Or, perhaps, 'confess' might be a better word."

This was followed by the three Marys, babbling at the same time and blaming each other for what happened to Meg, with Mary Beth being the most vocal. And Mary Catherine sobbing, and repeating over and over, "She wasn't supposed to die. No one intended for her to die."

"Everyone calm down," Sister Rose ordered, glaring at us so we all knew she meant business. "And please, don't all speak at once. Neecy," she said, "hand me that notebook. I will keep it for the time being, until we get this mess sorted out."

Having successfully restored what passed for order in my dining room, Sister Rose cleared her throat. Then demanded, "What happened at Fairport Manor the night before the reunion? How did Meg die? I want the truth."

Her facial expression made it crystal clear that nobody was going anywhere until she got it.

Mary Beth looked at the other members of the Golden Circle Club. And sighed. "Ok, Sister, I'll be the spokesperson." Then she glared at Claire. "But first, I want to know how you got your hands on that notebook. I thought it was…."

"Stolen?" I finished the sentence for her. "You mean, you had the nerve to sneak into my house and take it?"

"Don't be ridiculous, Carol," Mary Beth snapped. "I was at the Prentiss fundraiser the whole evening. You saw me."

"That's true," I said, "but you could have called someone to do your dirty work. And how would you know that the yellow notebook was taken, and when, if you had nothing to do with it?"

I was impressed with my logical thought process. I hope you are, too.

Mary Beth shot me a poisonous glance. "I resent your accusation, Carol. I don't have to tell you anything."

"By the way, Mary Beth," Claire said, pointing to the yellow notebook, "this happens to be my notebook, not yours. I figured if I used it today, somebody would react. And I was right. You did."

Sister Rose rapped on the table. "Let's get back to the main subject. I am asking you again. What happened to Meg the night before the reunion? How did she die?" I noticed that she shied away from using the word "murder." I didn't blame her.

"I'll tell you," Mary Ann said, glaring at Mary Beth. "I just want to get this out in the open, once and for all. When we heard about that filthy book, *Fifty Shades of Navy*, we never dreamed that Meg was the author. But we should have realized it, knowing her. It wasn't until we found out that Sister Rose had been sent an advance copy that the pieces started to fit together."

"Meg called each of us the week before the reunion and bragged about writing *Fifty Shades of Navy*," Mary Catherine said. "She claimed the book was going to make her rich."

"She used some of our old notebooks from the Golden Circle Club and embellished them, to publish this...filth," Mary Beth said. "And she told us she'd dedicated the book to us, and listed all our names. Her plan was to show up at the reunion, hand out copies of the book to everyone in our class, and humiliate us. Because we didn't stick up for her on the planning committee. What a witch."

Mary Catherine took up the story. "We were pretty desperate. We had to stop her. We'd kept the secret of the Golden Circle Club all these years, and couldn't risk exposure now. So we made a date to meet Meg at Mount Saint Francis the night before the reunion."

"Yeah, we actually thought we could talk her out of her plan," Mary Beth said. "I even brought a pitcher of Pink Squirrels, for old times' sake. We thought that getting together, like the old days, would make Meg change her mind.

"But instead, she laughed. She was going to the reunion and tell everybody about her book and the Golden Circle Club. Our reputations would be ruined. And, probably, our marriages, too."

"When we left Meg, she was alive," Neecy insisted, finally speaking up. "She was a little tipsy from the Pink Squirrels, but she was alive. We didn't do anything to cause her death. I don't understand what happened. I've gone over it and over it in my mind, and I just can't figure out what happened."

She looked at me. "That's why I wanted you to figure it out. But I never expected...this."

"Oh, God, what if we did do something? We didn't mean to. We really didn't." Now Mary Beth was sobbing.

Sheesh. We were getting nowhere. Well, we were getting somewhere, but I had no idea where. If that makes any sense to you.

"I thought Meg and I were best friends when we first met," Neecy said, stroking Porter's head in an effort to regain her composure. "And she was Anthony's godmother."

"Some godmother," J.T. said. I was startled to hear J.T. speak. Truthfully, I'd forgotten she was even in the room. "Anthony was my only love. We pledged to be together forever."

J.T. choked back a sob. "Meg ruined his life, your life and mine, Neecy. You never figured that out, did you? I hated her. More than the rest of you can ever imagine."

J.T. took a deep breath and looked straight at Neecy. "Your dear friend Meg killed your son. So I killed her. No, that's not right. I *executed* her.

"And after all these years, Anthony finally got the justice he deserved."

Neecy's face was white. "What do you mean, Meg killed my son?"

"Oh, for heaven's sake, Neecy," J.T. said in disgust. "Who do you think got him hooked on drugs in the first place? Didn't you ever wonder about all those weekend trips he took to New York City? About what he was doing there, or who he was meeting? She was his original supplier, until he got so hooked he graduated to hardcore drugs, like heroin. Meg was a real godmother, all right."

"I can't believe it," Mary Ann said.

"The woman was pure evil," J.T. said. "She never forgave you for marrying Tony, Neecy. Getting Anthony hooked on drugs was her revenge."

J.T. looked at the three Marys. "Maybe Meg wanted to humiliate all of you by handing out copies of *Fifty Shades of Navy*. But she wanted to destroy Neecy. Because Neecy had everything that Meg always wanted. Especially Tony."

Neecy buried her head in Porter's warm doggy coat and sobbed. The rest of us sat there, watching the sad scene and not quite knowing what to do next.

Until finally, Sister Rose said, "Carol, I think it's time to call the police."

Chapter 43

One nice thing about living in a small town is that when you don't know what you're doing, someone else usually does.

I don't think I'll ever be able to forget the sight of J.T. being led to a Fairport Police car by my own son-in-law. After she'd made her surprising confession, J.T. shut down completely, not offering any more information or explanation about Meg's death.

I wondered how much of what J.T. said was the truth, and how much was conjecture on her part. And I wondered, too, if we'd ever know that answer.

Naturally, Mark clammed up and refused to share anything with me about J.T.'s arrest. Although he did thank me for pointing the police (once again) in the right direction.

To everyone's surprise, J.T. pleaded guilty at her arraignment and waived her right to a trial by jury. And, despite the fact that her attorney tried to shush her, insisted on telling the judge how Meg died. It turned out that J.T. knew all about the famous Pink Squirrel cocktail that was the official drink of the Golden Circle Club. And because she was the marketing director at Fairport Manor, it was easy for her to pay an already inebriated Meg a surprise visit with another round of Pink Squirrels after the Marys and Neecy had left.

J.T.'s recipe had one extra ingredient, however: enough crushed Vicodin pills to be fatal, which were disguised in the creamy drink.

After Meg died, J.T. put her body on the bed, took away the incriminating cocktail shaker, substituted the pill bottle, and carefully arranged the suicide scene. Complete with the note, "Forgive me." The

Fairport police ruled Meg's death a suicide, and voila – Meg's remains were transported out of town and buried with no one being the wiser.

Except me, of course.

I had to admit, the note was a nice touch. But it also was a tip-off to all of us who really knew Meg that something was fishy.

J.T. refused to say why she'd picked *my* room (well, Nancy's and mine) for Meg's demise. I have my theories, but since I have no proof, I'm not going to tell you.

I heard through the classmate grapevine that J.T. is serving out her sentence at a women's prison on the Connecticut shoreline. Which makes it convenient for Neecy to visit her. Sometimes, she brings Porter, who is now a trained therapy dog.

By the way, Tony Prentiss lost the state senate election by a handful of votes. Which just goes to prove that Jim is absolutely right about the electoral process – every single vote counts.

The uproar around *Fifty Shades of Navy* faded away quickly. With no one – that would be the mysterious author – to promote it, people lost interest.

Every now and then, I see one of the Marys around Fairport. We smile, nod politely, and go our separate ways. Which is just fine with me.

Claire, Nancy, Mary Alice and I are even closer now than we were before, if you can believe it. Claire is putting pressure on all of us to buy condos in Florida for the winter. I don't know if I could ever convince Jim to spring for one, unless it's at a rock bottom price and, perhaps, is within walking distance to his favorite place.

No, not the beach. CVS.

Meanwhile, Jim and I are muddling along. Back to dullsville, as my dear mother used to say. I'm trying not to interfere in my children's lives, but I always check Jenny's tummy for any telltale bulge when she pops in for a quick visit. So, sue me.

I'm sure she'll confide in me when she and Mark decide to start a family. And it's a complete lie that I spend part of most days Googling sites like "How To Be A Perfect Grandmother" and picking out baby names.

But hey, I want to be prepared.

Mike checks in every now and then. He was a little disappointed that his Internet sleuthing skills didn't crack the case. Ah, well, maybe the next time.

Did I really say that? Jim has threatened to take away my credit cards if I get involved in another mystery.

Stay tuned.

Girls and Bullying

According to the National Crime Prevention Council (www.ncpc.org/topics/bullying/girls-and-bullying): When most people picture a "typical" bully, they imagine a boy who is bigger or older than his classmates, who doesn't do well in school, who fights, and who likes it when others are scared of him. Girls usually face a different type of bully, one who may not look as scary from the outside but who can cause just as much harm.

The typical girl who bullies is popular, well-liked by adults, does well in school, and can even be friends with the girls she bullies. She doesn't get into fist fights, although some girls who bully do. Instead, she spreads rumors, gossip, excludes others, shares secrets, and teases girls about their hair, weight, intelligence, and athletic ability. She usually bullies in a group and others join in or pressure her to bully.

This kind of bullying can have just as serious consequences as physical bullying. It can cause a drop in grades, low self-esteem, anxiety, depression, drug use, and poor eating habits in girls who are bullied. This kind of bullying is harder to see. Most of the time, adults don't realize when girls are being bullied in this way.

One of the best ways to stop this form of bullying is for the girls who see it or who are stuck in the middle to speak up and say that it is not ok. But only 15 percent of girls speak up, usually because they're afraid the bully will turn on them next. Parents and other adults can help girls beat bullying by teaching them how to stand up for themselves and their friends and by taking action themselves.

Here are a few things to remember:

- Encourage kids to be kind and to help others, particularly if they see someone being bullied. Praise them when they do so.
- Tell girls they are special, and point out why.
- Help girls get involved in activities outside of school so they can make friends in different social circles.

- Stop bullying when you see it. Don't let anyone, even your daughter, make fun of someone else, even if she says she is only joking.
- Be a good example. Don't gossip or make fun of others in front of young girls.
- If you know bullying is happening at school, speak to school officials and ask what they are doing to stop it.

National Bullying Prevention Month is a campaign begun in 2006 in the United States. The campaign was founded by PACER's National Center for Bullying Prevention, is held in October, and is promoted by social media sites such as Facebook, CNN, and Yahoo! Kids.

Several celebrities have begun anti-bullying campaigns, notably Lady Gaga, who founded her Born This Way foundation in 2012. Talk show host Ellen DeGeneres is also a fierce proponent of anti-bullying, as is Cape Cod singer Siobhan Magnus, an *American Idol* finalist, who wrote "Pure Inspiration" as an anti-bulling song and donates 50 percent of the record's profits to the Cape and Islands United Way for its anti-bullying program fund.

Planning a class reunion?

The Internet is filled with helpful sites to get you started. Notably www.classmates.com, www.reunionplanninghelp.com/Guide, and www.classquest.com. Websites for every graduating class of every high school are hosted by www.classreport.org, with free access for all class members. Believe it or not, over one million classes are now online. Another excellent resource is *Reunions Magazine* – www.reunionsmag.com, a quarterly publication designed to help in the planning of all types of reunions – family, class, even military. This site also has a reunions e-newsletter.

Some planners suggest at least a year to plan a class reunion.

Have fun, and don't forget the nametags!

Ruby Reunion Buffet – Forty Years Ago and Today

The average difference between the two styles of cooking is a minimum of 400 calories saved to over 1200 calories saved. The average portions are 4-6 per recipe. The main difference is between using whole dairy products with cream and the non-fat skim version. This includes milk, cream cheese, sour cream, and hard cheeses. Other changes are the shift from fully loaded mayonnaise to the non-fat version. The third biggest difference is the substitution of lettuce leaves and French endive leaves for bread.

The cheese cake is 77 calories for a 1 inch square by 2 inches high, one bite. If you can stop there, it's fine!

Menu

Sausage Stuffed Mushrooms

Cheese Puffs with Crab

Curry Olive Cheese Toasts

Prawn Cocktail

Bacon-Wrapped Scallops and Pineapple (or Water Chestnut) with Cherry Pepper Sauce

Smoked Salmon Rolls

Steak Diane

BBQ Pork Sliders with BBQ Slaw

Chicken Divan

Porcupine Balls

Seven Deadly Sins Cheesecake

WHAT WE GREW UP WITH:

Veal and Mascarpone Stuffed Mushrooms

Clean and remove stems of

16 extra-large white mushrooms

Mince stems with

2 cloves garlic and

3 scallions (white and green parts)

Remove casings and crumble

½ pound veal sausage (Bratwurst)

In a sauté pan, heat

2 T olive oil

2 T butter

Add and sauté for 5-7 minutes

Mushroom stems with garlic and onion

Veal Sausage

Remove from heat; add and stir until creamy

½ c panko crumbs

4 oz Mascarpone cheese

Mix in

¼ c grated Parmesan cheese

¼ c grated Romano or Asiago cheese

Salt and Pepper to taste

Fill each mushroom cap with mixture.

Arrange on baking sheet in single layer.

Bake at 350 degrees for 30 minutes.

Serve warm. Serves 8-12

REVISED REUNION VERSION:

Chicken Sausage Stuffed Mushrooms

Clean and remove stems from

16 extra-large white mushrooms

Mince stems with

2 cloves garlic and

3 scallions (white and green parts)

Remove casings and crumble

½ pound chicken sausage Italian style

Spray sauté pan with Pam or other spray olive oil.

Add and sauté for 5 minutes

Mushroom stems with garlic and onion

Chicken Sausage

Remove from heat; add and stir until creamy

½ c panko crumbs

2 oz lite cream cheese

Mix in

½ c lite Four Cheese Italian mix

Salt and Pepper to taste

Fill each mushroom cap with mixture.

Arrange on baking sheet in single layer.

Bake at 350 degrees for 30 minutes.

Serve warm. Serves 8-12

What we grew up with:

Cheese Puffs Stuffed with Crab

In sauce pan, heat till bubbles form around the edges

½ c whole milk

4 T unsalted butter (1/2 stick)

1 t salt

⅛ t white pepper

Then add all at once, stir constantly and cook for 2 minutes

½ c flour

2 extra large eggs, beaten

½ c grated Parmesan cheese

The dough should begin to form a ball and pull away from the sides of the pan.

Remove from heat.

Drop by tablespoons on baking sheets covered with parchment paper.

Bake 425 degrees for 15 minutes, then turn oven down to 350 degrees.

Remove and cool. Makes about 20 puffs.

Crab filling

Mix

2 oz cream cheese

1 T mayo

4 T sour cream

¼ t salt

⅛ t paprika

⅛ t onion powder

dash Worcestershire sauce

1 T pimento pepper chopped fine

6-8 oz crab

Cut puffs open like a bun; fill with crab mix.

Return to oven for 5-7 minutes.

Serve warm.

Revised Reunion Version:

Cheese Puffs Stuffed with Crab

In sauce pan, heat till bubbles form around the edges

½ c skim milk

4 T butter substitute of choice

1 t salt

⅛ t white pepper

Then add all at once, stir constantly and cook for 2 minutes

½ c whole wheat pastry flour

3 egg whites or egg substitute for 2 eggs

½ c grated Parmesan cheese

The dough should begin to form a ball and pull away from the sides of the pan.

Remove from heat.

Drop by tablespoons on baking sheets covered with parchment paper.

Bake 425 degrees for 15 minutes, then turn oven down to 350 degrees.

Remove and cool. Makes about 20 puffs.

Crab filling

Mix

2 oz lite cream cheese

1 T low fat mayo

4 T no fat sour cream

¼ t salt

⅛ t paprika

⅛ t onion powder

dash Worcestershire sauce

1 T pimento pepper chopped fine

6-8 oz crab

Cut puffs open like a bun, fill with crab mix.

Return to oven for 5-7 minutes.

Serve warm.

What we grew up with:

Curry Olive Cheese Toasts

Chop fine

1 c black olives

½ c green olives with pimento

¼ c green onions

Add and mix well

2 c grated cheddar cheese

½ c mayonnaise

¾ t yellow curry powder

Spread on small squares of ***rye bread.***

Place on single layer on baking sheet.

Bake at 400 degrees for 5-7 minutes.

Serve warm or at room temperature.

Revised Reunion Version:

Curry Olive Cheese Toasts

Chop fine

1 c black olives

½ c green olives with pimento

¼ c green onions

Add and mix well

2 c grated lite cheddar cheese

½ c low fat mayonnaise

¾ t yellow curry powder

Spread on small squares of ***rye bread.***

Place on single layer on baking sheet.

Bake at 400 degrees for 5-7 minutes.

Serve warm or at room temperature.

This recipe would not change:

Prawn Cocktail

Seasoned Prawns

Bring to boil in large pot and simmer 3-5 minutes

6 c water

3 T Old Bay seasoning

Add (with or without shells)

2-3 pounds large shrimp

Bring back to boil, let boil 3 minutes.

Turn off heat and let set 15 minutes.

Drain and cool.

Cape Cod Cocktail Sauce

Mix

2 T horseradish

1 t brown sugar or molasses

¼ t lemon juice

1 c sweet chili sauce

¼ t Dijon mustard

1/16 t chili paste

1 dash Worcestershire sauce

Serve on platter so prawn can be dipped into sauce.

What we grew up with:

Bacon-wrapped Scallops with Pineapple (or Water Chestnuts) and Cherry Pepper Sauce

Scallops

Clean and cut in half

1 pound large sea scallops

Remove from wrapper

¾-1 pound bacon

Open ***1 can whole water chestnuts*** and drain.

Open ***1 can of pineapple chunks*** and cut pieces in half.

Place piece of scallop and piece of pineapple or water chestnut together.

Wrap with strip of bacon and fasten together with toothpick through the middle.

In single layer on greased cookie sheet, broil for 10-12 minutes.

Brush with sauce halfway into the broiling time.

Turn once at about 6-7 minutes and brush with sauce again.

Cherry Pepper Sauce

In food processor, puree

½ c maraschino cherry juice

½ c cherries

½ c white sugar

½ c vinegar

⅛ t white pepper

Place in sauce pan and heat.

Mix ***1 T cornstarch*** with ***3 T water***.

Bring to simmer and cook until thick.

Cool slightly.

Brush on scallops halfway through the cooking time.

Revised Reunion Version:

Bacon-wrapped Scallops with Pineapple (or Water Chestnuts) and Cherry Pepper Sauce

Scallops

Clean and cut in half

1 pound large sea scallops

Remove from wrapper

¾-1 pound turkey bacon

Open ***1 can whole water chestnuts*** and drain.

Open ***1 can of pineapple chunks*** in own juice and cut pieces in half.

Place piece of scallop and piece of pineapple or water chestnut together.

Wrap with strip of bacon and fasten together with toothpick through the middle.

In single layer on greased cookie sheet, broil for 10-12 minutes.

Brush with sauce halfway into the broiling time.

Turn once at about 6-7 minutes and brush with sauce again.

Cherry Pepper Sauce

In food processor puree

½ c maraschino cherry juice

½ c cherries

¼ c Agave syrup

½ c vinegar

⅛ t white pepper

Place in sauce pan and heat.

Mix ***1 T cornstarch*** with ***3 T water***.

Bring to simmer and cook until thick.

Cool slightly.

Brush on scallops halfway through the cooking time.

What we grew up with:

Smoked Salmon Rolls

Hard boil, cool and chop fine

3 eggs

Pulse in good processor until minced

1 medium sweet onion

Add and combine until smooth

1 8 oz room temperature package cream cheese

¼ t garlic powder

1 t lemon juice

½ t dill weed

dash Worcestershire sauce

Place in bowl and combine with chopped egg.

Open package of ***8-10 oz smoked salmon.***

Place filling mix in layer on salmon filet.

Roll like jelly roll, wrap in plastic tightly.

Refrigerate to set.

With very sharp knife, cut the roll into pinwheel slices.

In single layer place on plate and return to refrigerator until ready to serve.

Place a slice on a cracker, sprinkle with ***paprika*** and serve with ***small dollop of sour cream.*** Can also be served on a lettuce leaf or a slice of cucumber.

Revised Reunion Version:

Smoked Salmon Rolls

Hard boil, cool and chop fine

3 eggs

Pulse in good processor until minced

1 medium sweet onion

Add and combine until smooth

1 8 oz room temperature package lite cream cheese

¼ t garlic powder

1 t lemon juice

½ t dill weed

dash Worcestershire sauce

Place in bowl and combine with chopped egg.

Open package of ***8-10 oz smoked salmon.***

Place filling mix in layer on salmon filet.

Roll like jelly roll, wrap in plastic tightly.

Refrigerate to set.

With very sharp knife cut the roll into pinwheel slices.

In single layer, place on plate and return to refrigerator until ready to serve.

Place a slice on a cracker, sprinkle with ***paprika*** and serve with ***small dollop of sour cream.*** Can also serve on a lettuce leaf or a slice of cucumber.

What we grew up with:

Steak Diane Sandwiches

Sauté until just soft

2 T butter

1 medium onion, chopped

1 carrot, grated

Add and form roux

2 T flour

Cook slightly.

Add

1 pint beef stock

1 bay leaf

¼ t thyme

1 stalk celery

3 stalks parsley

1 T tomato paste

1 t salt

½ t Worcestershire

Simmer until reduced by half – about 30 minutes.

Strain sauce, removing veggies and herbs.

Return sauce to pan and reduce further.

Add ***2 T brandy***, and flame pan with sauce.

Toss ***1 pound thinly sliced roast beef*** into sauce.

Bring just back to simmer.

Place beef with juices on ***hard roll.***

Serve with extra sauce on the side.

Revised Reunion Version:

Steak Diane Lettuce Wraps

Sauté until just soft

2 T butter

1 medium onion, chopped

1 carrot, grated

Add and form roux

2 T flour

Cook slightly.

Add

1 pint beef stock

1 bay leaf

¼ t thyme

1 stalk celery

3 stalks parsley

1 T tomato paste

1 t salt

½ t Worcestershire

Simmer until reduced by half – about 30 minutes.

Strain sauce, removing veggies and herbs.

Return sauce to pan and reduce further.

Add ***1 t brandy***.

Toss ***1 pound thinly sliced roast beef*** into sauce.

Bring just back to simmer.

Let meat cool.

Wrap in ***lettuce leaves***, refrigerate

Serve chilled.

What we grew up with:

BBQ Pork Sliders with BBQ Slaw

Pork

In crock pot place

3-4 pound pork roast
2 onions, finely chopped
2 cloves garlic, minced
1 c chicken stock
1 c white wine
12 oz BBQ sauce

Cook on low 8-10 hours.

Remove roast from pot.

With two forks pull meat apart.

Return to crockpot.

Slaw

Mix dressing

1 c mayo
4 oz BBQ sauce (same one used on pork)

Mix with 2-3 cups slaw mix ***or chopped cabbage and carrots.***

Put pork and sauce on bottom ***slider bun.***

Top with slaw and cover with top of bun.

Revised Reunion Version:

BBQ Pork Sliders with BBQ Slaw Endive Boats

Pork

In crock pot place

3-4 pound pork roast
2 onions, finely chopped
2 cloves garlic, minced
1 c chicken stock
1 c white wine
12 oz lite or low glycemic BBQ sauce

Cook on low 8-10 hours.

Remove roast from pot.

With two forks pull meat apart.

Return to crockpot and let cool.

Slaw

Mix dressing

1 c no fat mayo
4 oz lite or low glycemic BBQ sauce (same one used on pork)

Mix with 2-3 cups slaw mix ***or chopped cabbage and carrots.***

Layer 1-2 T pork in center of a ***French Endive leaf.***

Top with 1-2 T slaw, layer on tray, serve chilled.

WHAT WE GREW UP WITH:

Chicken Divan Rolls

Cook for 3 minutes in boiling water

1 pound broccoli or broccolini cut into small pieces – about ¼ to ½ inch

Drain.

In sauté pan form white roux

3 T butter

3 T flour

Add and stir until roux begins to thicken

1 c half and half warmed in microwave

Add and turn off heat

½ - ¾ c cheddar cheese

Salt and pepper to taste

Toss in broccoli pieces.

Remove from heat completely.

Take *2 pounds of thinly sliced chicken breast (chicken scallopini).*

In center of each slice place broccoli cream.

Roll up and fasten with toothpick.

Place in baking dish in single layer.

Cover with remaining broccoli cream.

Top with *more cheese* and *2 T bread crumbs.*

Bake at 400 degrees for 15 minutes, until bubbly.

Serve over *buttered noodles, or cut rolls in half* and keep in warming dish.

REVISED REUNION VERSION:

Chicken Divan on Lite Ritz Crackers

Cook for 3 minutes in boiling water

1 pound broccoli or broccolini, cut into small pieces – about ¼ to ½ inch

Drain.

Warm in microwave

1 c non-fat half and half

Make paste and then add

1 ½ T cornstarch

1 T water

Bring to simmer and stir until mixture starts to thicken.

Add and let melt

½ - ¾ c lite cheddar cheese

Salt and pepper to taste

Toss in broccoli pieces.

Remove from heat.

Take *2 pounds of thinly sliced chicken breast (chicken scallopini).*

In center of each slice, place broccoli cream.

Roll up and fasten with toothpick.

Place in baking dish in single layer.

Cover with remaining broccoli cream.

Top with *more cheese* and *2 T bread crumbs.*

Bake at 400 degrees for 15 minutes, until bubbly.

Let cool, slice into ½ - 1 inch rounds.

Place on *lite Ritz crackers.*

This would not change:

Porcupine Balls in Marinara Sauce

Meatballs

Cook ½ ***cup rice*** in ***1 c water*** for 40 minutes; let cool.

Combine

1 pound meatloaf mix

1 c cooked rice

1 egg, beaten

2 T chopped onions

1 T fresh parsley chopped

½ T oregano chopped

½ t salt

⅛ t pepper

Roll into meatballs.

Bake at 350 degrees for 20-30 minutes.

Marinara Sauce

Sauté

4 T olive oil

1 medium onion, chopped

2 cloves garlic, chopped

Add and simmer 10 minutes

1 bay leaf

1 c wine

1 large can tomato puree

Salt and pepper to taste

Add meatballs to sauce, cook for additional 10-12 minutes.

Serve with toothpicks.

Seven Deadly Sins Cheesecake

Note: Before filling the springform pan, wrap large piece of heavy foil around the outside bottom to make it airtight.

When the pan is filled with batter, place pan in a waterbath.

Cheesecakes need moisture to bake completely

First Layer

Crush

8 oz of shortbread cookies

Mix with

3 T melted, unsalted butter

1 t vanilla paste

2 T water

Press into bottom of springform pan.

Bake in lowest 1/3 of oven at 350 degrees for 10 minutes.

Remove, cool and refrigerate for 15 minutes.

Second Layer

Melt ***2 oz semisweet chocolate***

Pour onto crust, spread evenly and refrigerate for 10 minutes.

While that is chilling, make the next three layers.

Third Layer

In saucepan, combine

2½ c berries of choice (strawberries or raspberries are great)

½ c sugar

2½ T cornstarch

Cook until thick, crushing berries with back of spoon while cooking.

Cool completely.

Layer on chocolate and return to refrigerator.

Fourth Layer

Beat on medium till fluffy

1 8 oz package cream cheese

¼ c sugar

Add

1 egg

¼ t vanilla

Stir in

2 oz melted milk chocolate

⅓ c sour cream

Spoon over berry layer.

Fifth Layer

Beat till fluffy

1 8 oz package cream cheese

⅓ c brown sugar

1 T flour

Add

1 egg

½ t vanilla

¼ c chopped pecans

Gently spoon over pecan layer.

Sixth Layer

Beat together till fluffy

5 oz cream cheese

¼ c sugar

Add

1 egg

1 c sour cream

¼ t vanilla

¼ t almond extract

Bake in 325 degree oven for 1 hour. Do not open oven door yet.

Turn oven off, leave cake in for 30 minutes.

Open oven door and leave for additional 30 minutes. Let cake cool completely and chill for at least 8 hours, preferably overnight.

Seventh Layer

Melt

6 oz semisweet chocolate

¼ c butter

Add

¾ c powdered sugar

2 T sweet liquor of choice

1 T vanilla

Spread glaze over cake, return to refrigerator to chill completely.

Cut with sharp knife that is wiped clean after each cut.

Enjoy!

Pink Squirrel

¾ oz Amaretto or Crème de Almond

¾ oz white Crème de Cacao

1½ oz heavy cream

Shake over ice, strain into chilled martini glass.

Iced Pink Squirrel

1 part Crème de Almond or Amaretto

1 part white Crème de Cacao

2 parts vanilla ice cream

Mix in blender, garnish with cherry and serve in chilled martini glass.

Chef Paulette DiAngi is an international award winning Vintner, food alchemist and Ayurvedic Lifestyle Consultant. She indulged her passion for cooking at the Connecticut Culinary Institute after receiving her PhD in Nursing from Case Western Reserve University. Her goal is to create food to 'fall in love with' that engages all the senses. In addition to her day job and two TV shows (Paulette's Red Kitchen and Love On A Plate), she teaches at Sandwich (MA) Community School and provides private lessons in her kitchen or yours. Email her at: www.paulettesredkitchen.com.

About the Author

Susan Santangelo

An early member of the Baby Boomer generation, **Susan Santangelo** has been a feature writer, drama critic and editor for daily and weekly newspapers in the New York metropolitan area, including a stint at *Cosmopolitan* magazine. A seasoned public relations and marketing professional, she has designed and managed not-for-profit events and programs for over 25 years, and was principal of her own public relations firm, Events Unlimited, in Princeton NJ for ten years. She also served as Director of Special Events and Volunteers for Carnegie Hall during the Hall's 1990-1991 Centennial season.

Susan divides her time between Cape Cod, MA and the Connecticut shoreline. She is a member of Sisters in Crime and the Cape Cod Writers Center, and also reviews mysteries for Suspense magazine. She shares her life with her husband Joe and one very spoiled English cocker spaniel, Boomer, who also serves as the model for the books' covers.

A portion of the sales from the Baby Boomer Mysteries is donated to the Breast Cancer Survival Center, a non-profit organization based in Connecticut which Susan founded in 1999 after being diagnosed with cancer herself.

You can contact Susan at ssantangelo@aol.com
Or find her on Facebook and Twitter.
She'd love to hear from you.

Attention Book Clubs

If you have made ***Retirement Can Be Murder, Moving Can Be Murder, Marriage Can Be Murder*** or ***Class Reunions Can Be Murder*** your book club selection and would like to have Susan Santangelo discuss the book with your group, please send an e-mail to ssantangelo@aol.com and we'll do our best to accommodate you.